TO HEAL THE

St Paul's Church, Mount Argus. To the right is the old church where Saint Charles prayed and blessed the sick.

Paul Francis Spencer CP

To Heal the Broken Hearted

THE LIFE OF SAINT CHARLES OF MOUNT ARGUS

He has sent me to bring good news to the poor,
to bind up hearts that are broken

Isaiah 61:1

OVADA

2007

Published in the United Kingdom by

OVADA BOOKS

Saint Mungo's Retreat, 52 Parson Street
Glasgow, G4 0RX

Tel/Fax +44 (0)141 552 5523

ISBN 978-1-905965-02-1

www.ovadabooks.com
info@ovadabooks.com

Originally published by Gill & Macmillan, 1988
Published in a revised edition by © Ovada Books, 2007

Database right Ovada Books (maker)
All rights reserved

Cum permissu superiorum

A Catalogue record for this book is available from the British Library

Printed in Glasgow by Bell & Bain Ltd
www.bell-bain.co.uk
∞

In Memory of Declan O'Sullivan CP

1903–1981

Scriba doctus in regno cælorum
qui profert de thesauro sua
nova et vetera

Contents

At the end of Saint Mark's Gospel, Jesus says, 'Go out into the whole world and proclaim the Good News'. On first reading, we might think that this is about preaching the Gospel in the sense of standing up and talking about Jesus. But words are not the only way of proclaiming the Good News.

Saint Charles of Mount Argus knew about another kind of proclamation. Although no great preacher, he was able to communicate the good news of Jesus Christ in a different way. His life was a life of service to those in need of God. He was always ready to respond to the sick and the suffering, the lonely, the poor and broken hearted. Charles knew how to communicate the compassionate love of Christ and the healing blessing of the presence of God. While his hours in the monastery were spent in silent communion with God, he was prompt to answer the call of the distressed. The people who still come to Mount Argus to seek his intercession, more than a hundred years after his death, testify to the effectiveness of his proclamation of the Good News.

'Preach the Gospel; use words when necessary' said Saint Francis of Assisi (I am indebted to James Martin's *My Life with the Saints* for this quotation). It was not by words but by his way of living that Saint Charles preached his message. As a Passionist, he had vowed to keep alive in his own heart and in the hearts of others the memory of the life-giving Passion of Jesus. He carried that memory in his own heart through daily meditation. He brought the remembrance of Christ's Passion to others by giving them hope in their sufferings. Not all the people he blessed were cured physically; the healing love which flows from the Cross can work on different levels. Although hundreds of people were cured in his lifetime, and others after his death, in many cases the healing which God gives through Charles' intercession was and is of a quieter kind, though no less real: the grace to accept a terminal illness; the strength to keep going in the face of disability; the power to forgive one who has hurt us deeply; the courage to accept help in overcoming an addiction; the sense of God's closeness in difficult times.

By a happy coincidence, the year of Charles' canonisation is also the one hundred and fiftieth anniversary of his first arrival in Ireland. John Andrew Houben, the Dutchman, became Charles of Saint Andrew, the Passionist. He is known to us as Saint Charles of Mount Argus; the name of what was then the newly-founded Passionist monastery has become firmly linked to his. Saint Paul's Retreat, Mount Argus was his home and the centre of his apostolate for more than thirty years. It was also to be his final resting place.

Like Saint Patrick, he learned to love the Irish as his own people; they in turn took him to their hearts. The old Irish tradition is that the stranger should be welcomed as we would welcome Christ. In Charles' case, the presence of Christ was easy for people to recognise, as he, who lived always in the awareness of God's loving presence, touched the lives of so many with the healing grace of a loving God.

May Charles' silent preaching continue to be Good News for us all.

Paul Francis Spencer CP

The publication of this book coincides with the beatification of the man usually known as 'Fr Charles of Mount Argus'. Born in Limburg, Holland, in 1821, John Andrew Houben entered the Passionist Novitiate in 1845, receiving the name Charles of Saint Andrew; in the official documents of the Cause this is the name we find, but for most people the name of Blessed Charles is linked indissolubly with that of the monastery in which he lived for almost thirty years and in whose church his body lies: Saint Paul's Retreat, Mount Argus.

One of the difficulties confronting the biographer of Blessed Charles is the scarcity of information, particularly for the early years of his life as a religious and a priest. It is only in the last twenty years of his life that we find an abundance of documentation. One of his contemporaries described his life as 'quiet and hidden for the sake of Him for whom alone he lives'; the truth of this statment is reflected in the archives of many of the houses in which he lived. This book, the content of which is taken from primary sources, reflects in its structure the material available.

My intention in writing this biography of Blessed Charles has been to allow the story to be told by those who were there: Charles himself and those who knew him. To this end, I have tried to intrude as little as possible, letting the documents speak for themselves. In the pages which follow I have spoken of our subject as Charles, rather than Blessed Charles; knowing that he used to refer to himself as Charlie, I feel sure he won't mind.

It is my hope that the reader will be helped to see Blessed Charles as he was, a man of God seeking to do the will of God, but at the same time a human being living in a very human situation. It was my own experience that, as I came to know him better through reading the various documents, I felt drawn to him not by the extraordinary aspects of his life but simply by the love and compassion which were so clearly expressed in all his activities. I hope you will have that same experience.

I wish to thank all who helped in the preparation of this book, in particular the following: Father Pancras Fanning CP, Archivist, Saint Paul's Retreat, Mount Argus; Father Paulinus Vanden Bussche CP, Archivist, Province of Saint Gabriel (Belgium); Father Ignatius McElligott CP, Archivist, Province of Saint Joseph, England; Father Paulino Alonso Blanco CP, General Archivist, Father Carlos Lizarraga CP, Postulator General and Father Fabiano Giorgini CP, SS. Giovanni e Paolo, Rome; also David Sheehy of the Dublin Diocesan Archives and his predecessor, Father Kevin Kennedy.

I am also grateful to Sister Mary Woodall, of the Little Company of Mary, for the Appendix on the *Positio super Miraculo*, and to Sean Goan, who read the manuscript and whose companionship and encouragement helped me to finish the job. However, the one, under God, who deserves most credit for the completion of this book is Father Oliver Kelly CP, Vice Postulator. In the six years since we first discussed this project Father Oliver's interest and enthusiasm were a constant inspiration. To him I am deeply grateful.

October 1988

I

Glory and Thanks be to God

OUR STORY BEGINS, as no well-told story should, at its conclusion; what will follow is in a sense simply an explanation of this conclusion, which is also a beginning. Our story opens then with a letter written by the Rector of Mount Argus, Dublin, to Anne Mary Lenssen, Munstergeleen, on 12 January 1893, to inform her of her brother's death.

Madam,
It is with the deepest regret that I write to you, to give you the sad news of the death of good Father Charles. He passed from this life on the 5th of this month. His death, like his life, was that of a saint. During the whole time that his body lay in the church, crowds of people were filing past constantly, in order to have their rosaries and other objects of devotion touched against his body. There was an enormous multitude at his funeral. Nobody wanted to pray for his soul; on the contrary, all were ready to ask his intercession. It is true to say that in the opinion of the people he is already canonised. Please accept my condolences, Madam, on this occasion.

> Your servant in Jesus Christ,
>
> Dominic O'Neill, Rector

What Anne Mary's reaction to this was would be hard to imagine; it was sad news indeed, but surprising news too: the death of 'good Father Charles', her brother Andrew; a death like that of a saint; canonised in the minds of the people. She had not seen her brother for nearly fifty years. When he left home to join the Passionists, she was only fourteen years old. Anne Mary had often seen the words her father had written in his prayer book the day Andrew was born: 'John Andrew Houben was born 11 December 1821. Glory and thanks be to God'. In her own mind she added, 'Father Charles of Saint Andrew died 5 January 1893. Glory and thanks be to God'.

The village of Munstergeleen lies in the Dutch province of Limburg, where Holland meets the borders of Germany and Belgium. Here it was that in the second half of the eighteenth century Arnold Houben from Limbrecht had come to find work. He was taken on at the flour mill and so it happened that, after a few years, Arnold married the miller's daughter. When his father-in-law died, the mill passed on to Arnold and his wife, Mary Sibyl.

In 1795 Arnold Houben died at the age of forty-four, leaving Mary Sibyl with eight children of whom the oldest, Mary Gertrude, was twenty-three and the youngest, Mary Christine, only a year old. The work at the mill was taken over by the oldest son, Peter Arnold. He was twenty-one years old and had to take his father's place both at the mill and in the home, taking care of his brothers and sisters as well as the family business. Peter Arnold never married; as often happens in such circumstances, his brothers and sisters became, in a sense, his children.

One of Peter Arnold's younger brothers was also called Peter: Peter Joseph Houben, the father of Andrew, known to us as Charles. Peter Joseph was only five years old when his father died. When he grew older he learned to work with his brother at the mill, but he did not intend to remain a bachelor like Peter Arnold. At twenty-six he married a girl from the village, Johanna Elizabeth Luyten. Johanna was just a year younger than her husband, whose elder brother was happy to have them stay in the house at the flour mill. It was a big house and there would be plenty of room for everyone.

The newly-married couple did not forget Peter Arnold's kindness and when, a year later, their first son was born, they gave him his uncle's name. Four years later, a second son was born; he was called John Andrew after Johanna's brother, who was his godfather, but to the family he would be known simply as Andrew (see end of chapter).

On the day he was born Andrew was baptised by the parish priest of Munstergeleen, Father Peter Delahaye. The church in which he was baptised has since disappeared, but the stone baptismal font was preserved and can be seen in the present church, as can the baptismal register in which Father Delahaye wrote:

On 11 December 1821 was born and baptised John Andrew, lawful son of Peter Joseph Houben and Johanna Elizabeth Luyten. Sponsors: John Andrew Luyten and Mary Gertrude Deverin, as proxy for Mary Ida Houben of Einighausen in the parish of Limbrecht.

Andrew's first steps in this world were taken under the guidance of his mother and father and they were his first teachers in the faith, showing him how to pray and how to live. He never forgot his debt to them, as can be seen in a letter he wrote from Dublin seventeen years after leaving his family home; in the letter he prays for his married brother and sister, John Matthew and Anne Mary, that they may be like their parents, and in doing so he gives us a picture of his own childhood:

I pray for them, that if God grants them children, they will bring them up to know his peace, have them pray every morning and every night, and teach them to recite the Rosary in the evening, and that the welfare of their souls will be the most important thing in life for them. We should be thankful to God for having given us such good parents.

Another person who was to have a deep influence on young Andrew was Father John Christian Delahaye. He was appointed as parish priest of Munstergeleen on the death of his uncle, Father Peter Delahaye, when Andrew was just two years old; on 14 May 1824 he arrived from nearby Sittard, where he had been a curate. The new parish priest was full of enthusiasm for his work; he declared that he was prepared to get his parishioners to heaven, even if he had to drag them there by the hair of the head! His preaching on Death and the Last Judgment made a lasting impression on his hearers, and not least on Andrew.

Father Delahaye was a strong advocate of education; he promoted the work of the Confraternity for Christian Education, which Andrew was later to join. He encouraged parents to send their children to school and at one stage was able to say that out of six hundred parishioners, one hundred and twenty were attending school. Indeed so keen was he on this that he would not admit to First Communion any child who could not read and write.

As a boy Andrew attended the village primary school where, under the direction of Father Delahaye, he made his preparation for First Communion, which he received on the second Sunday of Easter, 26 April 1835; two months later, on 28 June, he was confirmed by Bishop Richard Anthony van Bommel. It was around this time that he became an altar server and also joined the Confraternity of Perpetual Adoration. Already at fourteen years of age he began to spend time adoring Jesus in the Eucharist. It became his usual practice to visit the Blessed Sacrament on his way home from school and often after services in the church he would remain behind to pray, so that at times his mother would have to send one of his brothers or sisters to bring him home for supper. Indeed, the family used to smile and say that Andrew knew only two roads, the road to school and the road to church. To those outside his family he seemed quiet and extremely shy, but within his own home he was always cheerful and full of life. His brothers and sisters described him as having been always content with everything and everybody, and they remembered how he used to go about the house singing as he worked. His sister Anne Mary would later tell her children that she wished they would try to be like their uncle Andrew who, at their age, knew the catechism well and always said his prayers.

After his First Communion and Confirmation, Andrew left the primary school and began attending classes at Sittard, two miles from his home. A secular priest, Father Kallen, had recently opened a High School in the old Dominican College buildings. Here Andrew was able to learn French and Latin, languages which would later be very useful to him. He worked as best he could at his studies, but the house did not provide a quiet setting for reading and writing. The noise of the mill together with the comings and goings of people from the village was a constant distraction to him. In addition, by this time the family home was bursting at the seams: there were ten children in the house, as well as their parents and Uncle Peter. Andrew's mother's brother, who was now Mayor of Munstergeleen, lived not too far away. He offered to let Andrew and his oldest sister Mary Sibyl stay in his house for a while. Sibyl could help about the house, while for Andrew, Mayor Luyten's would be a quiet place where he could study in peace; at the same time, it was only a few minutes' walk from their parents' home.

In the autumn of 1837, shortly after Sibyl and Andrew had moved into the Mayor's house, a new curate arrived in the village: Father Henry Gobbels was no stranger to the place, having been born at Geleen. He had been ordained on 13 August 1837, and the curacy at Munstergeleen was his first appointment. He was twenty-four years old, eight years older than Andrew. The new priest needed a place to stay; Mayor Luyten was happy to take him in.

Until now the only priest Andrew had known was Father

Delahaye, a man much older than himself and quite distant in his manner. Now he found himself living in the same house as a young, newly-ordained priest who, as well as being nearer his own age, was from this very place. As he chatted with Father Gobbels at the fireplace in the evenings or asked him for help with his homework, perhaps Andrew began to feel drawn to the priesthood not just as something to be admired but as a possible way of life.

Progress in the College at Sittard was slow; Andrew worked hard but, as Father Gobbels observed, he had great difficulty in learning, so much so that his parents tried to discourage him from continuing at the College. His mother, anxious for his health, would say to him, 'But Andrew, does all this studying not make you too tired? Would you not like to put your books away and help your father?' However, Andrew's quiet determination pushed him forward, supported no doubt by the kindness of Father Gobbels and Mayor Luyten. In later years he did not forget the help they had given him; writing to his uncle long afterwards, he says:

My dear uncle, I am endebted to you not just financially but in so many other ways too; I hope you will forgive me if I have failed to pay you back.

The months and the years passed by, and Andrew was still to be seen plodding along the road to Sittard, making progress in his studies steadily but very slowly, and at the same time not forgetting his visit to the church, growing steadily in his life of prayer. Somehow he knew that God wanted him to persevere in both of these; to what precise purpose he was not yet sure.

When Andrew was nineteen years old he was enrolled for military service in the First Infantry Regiment. Although enrolled on 2 March 1840 and not dismissed until 10 March 1845, he was in active service for only three months. Having made a general confession to Father Gobbels before leaving home, he arrived in the Markiezenkoph Barracks at Bergen-Op-Zoom on 9 July 1841. Here with the other new recruits he went through a programme of basic training. It was obvious to his companions that Andrew's heart was not set on a military career. They used to say that the miller's son would not make a good soldier because he spent too much time in church. It is said that on one occasion during his time as a soldier there was a disturbance in the town; the army were called out and ordered to fire. Afraid that he might hit some-one, Andrew pointed his rifle the wrong way and narrowly missed shooting his superior officer.

Whether this story is true or not, Andrew was certainly not thinking of spending the rest of his life in the army. His mind had started to move in another direction. His biographers tell us that it was while he was in the army that he first heard of the newly-established Passionist community at Ere in Belgium, through another conscript called Raaymakers, whose brother had been received into their novitiate. In fact Brother Anthony Raaymakers did not arrive at the Passionist house to become a novice until 2 August 1842, almost ten months after Andrew had finished his active service. Was he himself the conscript with whom Andrew discussed this new group of religious, recently arrived from Italy? How did either of them come to hear about this monastery which was hundreds of miles from their homes in the southern, French-speaking part of Belgium? Unfortunately we have no definite answer to either of these questions. However, we can put forward one possible sequence of events.

On 1 May 1841, the *Journal Historique et Littéraire*, a magazine published at Liège by a priest, Father Kersters, printed an article about the Passionists at Ere. The curate, Father Gobbels, who had been ordained at Liège, may well have received a copy of the magazine and given it to Andrew to read. The article appeared just five weeks before Andrew left home to begin his military service. It is possible that he arrived at Bergen-Op-Zoom with the idea of joining the Passionists already on his mind and that he found a sympathetic listener in his companion Raaymakers.

The article in the *Journal Historique et Littéraire* had stated that the Passionists had recently established a novitiate at Ere, near Tournai; it described their mission in these terms:

The purpose of this institute, founded by Venerable Paul of the Cross almost a hundred years ago, is to bring about the conversion of sinners. In particular the Passionists devote themselves to hearing confessions and giving retreats in villages, towns, seminaries and religious communities. In all their houses they receive priests and other gentlemen who wish to make retreats. They do not refuse to work among pagans and heretics whenever called upon to do so, and it could be said that this is their greatest wish.

The author described the lifestyle of the Passionists as being extremely austere: going barefoot, wearing sandals only; sleeping on straw mattresses; rising at midnight to chant Matins; devoting long periods of time to meditation every day.

This information, whether it came to him from the magazine article or from his fellow soldier, certainly gave Andrew something new to think about: a life of prayer and penance, in which he would be helping others to come close to God, with the possibility of going as a missionary to some other land to spread the Faith. As he sat in the army barracks with his friend Raaymakers discussing what they would do after their military service, he became more and more convinced that this was what God was asking of him: he would indeed be a soldier, but a soldier of Christ, under the banner of the Cross. Like other soldiers before him – Francis of Assisi, Ignatius Loyola and Paul of the Cross himself – he now realised that he was to put on the armour of the Lord.

On 9 October Andrew's period of active military service came to an end and he returned to Munstergeleen. On leaving home three months earlier, he had received from his parents a belt containing a sum of money which he now brought home intact; but he also brought home something which for him was of greater value, a sense of purpose. If he was to achieve that purpose and join the Passionist community, he would have to continue his studies, particularly Latin and French. The College at Sittard had been closed due to the death of Father Kallen, so Andrew turned to Mr Schrijen, a schoolmaster living at Broeksittard, who agreed to take him as a pupil. Now almost twenty years old, Andrew found in Mr Schrijen an excellent teacher and also a friend. He discussed with him his desire to become a Passionist. Mr Schrijen had heard about this community and he gave Andrew every encouragement. A remarkable change began to take place: the student who had been so slow and apparently stupid started to make rapid progress. Mr Schrijen himself described the difference between Andrew's previous school record and his newfound success as truly amazing. Andrew had gained two assets by which he discovered a new enthusiasm for education: a relationship of trust and understanding between himself and his teacher, and a specific aim towards which his studies were directed.

He was to spend another four years at home, studying with Mr Schrijen and, when he could, helping at the mill. His uncle Peter, who as a young man carried the burden of the family business, was gradually becoming more feeble and less fit for work. Finally on 17 January 1843 he died at the age of sixty-nine; he had been like a father to Peter Joseph, his younger brother, and to his nieces and nephews he had taken the place of the grandfather they had never known.

Uncle Peter's death was not the only sorrow to touch the Houben family during those years. Almost exactly a year later on 19 January 1844, Johanna Elizabeth Houben, Andrew's mother, died. She was just fifty-two years old; Andrew was twenty-two. The experience of the death of someone we love brings us face to face with the fragility of our human existence and can make us question the value of what we are doing with our lives. For young Andrew there must have been a struggle with this grief as he attempted to reconcile his feelings of loss with his faith in a loving God. Some fifteen years later, when his brother John Peter died, he wrote to his family:

He was so good, kind and loving to our family. His death must have caused you all great sorrow. Yet I am happy to hear from you that he led a most exemplary life.... Let us thus console each other and let us realise that it is the will of God, and that he died as one predestined, having been strengthened by the last sacraments.

We can easily apply these words to Andrew's mother and see in this letter the fruits of his own experience; he acknowledges the great sorrow that is felt and at the same time, without suppressing the pain, allows it to co-exist with the realisation that this is willed by God and is part of his plan for those whom he has predestined in love.

On 18 February 1845 Andrew's period as a reserve in the army came to an end and he was formally discharged. He was now free to take the step he had thought and prayed about for so long. He made contact with the Passionist community at Ere and informed them that he wished to enter the novitiate. It was agreed that he should arrive at the beginning of November.

When the time came for him to leave home, Andrew went to each of his brothers and sisters in turn to say goodbye; for each he had a word of encouragement or advice. His eldest sister Sibyl, who had been his companion during the years in his uncle's house, was afraid that in his heart Andrew would have preferred to stay at home; even she, who was perhaps closest to him found it hard at times to be sure of what he was thinking. 'Are you really going away of your own free will?' she asked. 'Ah Sibyl', Andrew replied, 'for our Lord I would do anything; I would even go and live at the bottom of a well'.

On that last evening at home the family sat down at the kitchen table to have supper together. It was a sad moment for his brothers and sisters; some of them began to cry. His father made a last vain attempt to hold on: 'Andrew, there's enough to eat for all of us; one more won't make any difference. You don't have to go away to that monastery'. Andrew answered quietly but firmly, 'I've said that I will go to the monastery and I'm going'. With a last embrace for his father and his brothers and sisters, he set out with his uncle, Mayor Luyten, on the journey to Ere. As they crossed the bridge to leave the village, Andrew stopped for a moment, looked back and said, 'Good-bye, Munstergeleen'.

Note

Peter Joseph Andrew Houben (born 15 February 1790) and Johanna Elizabeth Luyten (born 6 March 1791) had eleven children:
Peter Arnold, born 3 August 1817, died 30 July 1878; Mary Sibyl, born 28 October 1818, died 20 October 1896; Mary Christine, born 22 January 1820, died 26 April 1871; John Andrew, born 11 December 1821, died 5 January 1893; John Peter, born 25 May 1823, died 24 January 1859; John Matthew, born 26 May 1825, died 1 December 1907; Peter Joseph, born 9 February 1827, died 18 August 1883; Godfrey, born 9 June 1829, died 7 July 1892; Anne Mary, born 5 March 1831, died 5 March 1912; a tenth child, stillborn, 27 September 1833; Mary Helen, born 3 May 1835, died 23 March 1917.

II

Charles of Saint Andrew

Andrew Houben arrived at Ere on 5 November 1845. The Chateau d'Ere had belonged to Baroness de Croeser of Valenciennes, who had given the property to the Passionists as their first monastery outside Italy. With the arrival of four Passionists from Rome on 15 June 1840, the house was renamed Holy Cross Retreat; the word 'Retreat' was used by the founder of the Passionists, Saint Paul of the Cross, when referring to the houses of his Congregation, as exemplifying the spirit of prayer, penance and solitude which animates the Passionist life.

As a young man Saint Paul of the Cross had felt drawn to a life of contemplation, centred on the Passion of Jesus, but at the same time he believed that God was calling him to be a preacher of the Mystery of the Cross, sharing with others the message of God's infinite love which is revealed on Calvary. In 1720, at the age of twenty-six, Paul wrote a rule of life for a new community whose members would contemplate and proclaim the Mystery of the Cross. The Paschal Mystery of Christ's Death and Resurrection, source of life for all who believe, was symbolised for Paul in the distinctive dress of his community: a black habit on the front of which is the badge or sign of the Passionists – surmounted by a white cross, the symbol of a heart in which are inscribed the words 'the Passion of Jesus Christ'. In his writings he explains that when, as a young man, the form of the habit was revealed to him as he prayed, he heard these words of explanation: 'This signifies how pure and spotless that heart should be which must bear the holy name of Jesus graven upon it'.

Saint Paul of the Cross had a special love for 'England and the neighbouring kingdoms' of Ireland and Scotland. It was his hope that some day the Passionists would work there for the healing of the divisions between Christians, seeking unity under the Cross of Christ. His ecumenical vision and lifelong prayer bore fruit when Blessed Dominic Barberi, who had opened the house at Ere, set out for England with one companion in October 1841. When Andrew Houben arrived at Holy Cross Retreat four years later, everyone in the house would have been talking about England. Just three weeks earlier Blessed Dominic had arrived from Oxford with the news that he had received John Henry Newman into the Catholic Church, an event which proved to be not just the talk of the monastery but the talk of Europe. Naturally Andrew, on hearing this, would have been filled with enthusiasm for the English foundation and for the work of promoting Christian unity.

Before he could be received as a novice, Andrew spent a month as a postulant. The period of postulancy is a time in which the candidate is introduced to the community so that he can learn about its life and so that the community can judge whether or not he is suitable for acceptance as a novice. Before a young man would be admitted into the novitiate, Saint Paul of the Cross wished his patience and humility to be tested; in the sixth chapter of the Rule he wrote:

For this end he shall be publicly reprehended, particularly in the refectory, and shall sometimes eat upon the ground, and perform other humiliating and mortifying works ordered by the Superiors, from which it may be clearly known whether he has a real love of being despised; whether he be dead to himself and to the world, in order to live only to God, in God, and through God, willingly hiding his life in Jesus Christ, who, for our sakes, chose to become the reproach of men, and the outcast of the people, giving the most faultless example of all virtues.

At the end of his postulancy, on the recommendation of the Master of Novices, Father Valentine Guerrini, the community decided to accept Andrew as a novice. On the evening of 1 December, after Compline, he was clothed in the black habit of the Passion and given the name Charles. As one who would later study for the priesthood, he would be addressed as Confrater rather than Brother; for his devotional title he was permitted to keep the name of the patron he had since baptism: Andrew. From now on he would be known not as Andrew Houben but as Confrater Charles of Saint Andrew.

The seven years Charles spent as novice, student and student-priest represent the most hidden part of his life. These are years about which we know practically nothing. There have come down to us from this time none of his letters and only a few recollections of his companions. Yet these were the years in which the foundations of his future priestly and religious life were being laid; the grain of wheat lay buried in the ground, waiting to bear much fruit.

In the first months of his novitiate year, Charles was joined by other young men, including Isidore Brems who would later be Provincial of Belgium, France and Holland, and Michael Emons who was, like Charles, a former pupil of Mr Schrijen of Broeksittard. According to Michael, even as a young man Charles was 'always humble, simple, charitable and exact in the observance of the Rule. He was greatly loved by his superiors and companions because of his simplicity, humility and obedience'.

Blessed Dominic, who visited the community while Charles was a novice, was very happy with the way things were at Ere. He wrote to the General, Father Anthony Testa, on 29 September 1846, 'There are eight novices. Almost all seem to me to be quite good, expecially the six Dutch, who have an angelic nature'. Dominic went on to say that he was also pleased with the Novice Master; he found him quite lively, but, he added, 'that's not a crime!'

Towards the end of that year, on 10 December, Charles made his religious profession. The profession should have been earlier but it was delayed for a week or so because the superior, Father Peter Magagnotto, was in France giving a retreat to the Benedictines at Douai. At his profession, as well as the three vows of poverty, chastity and obedience, Charles took the distinctive vow of the Passionists, by which he committed himself to contemplating the mystery of Christ's suffering and promoting in the hearts of others the memory of the Passion. After pronouncing his vows he received the Passionist sign which, as a professed member of the Congregation, he would now wear on his habit.

Charles' remaining years at Ere were spent studying philosophy and theology. His teacher was Father Seraphin Giammaria, but the course which was followed was the work of Blessed Dominic, whose textbooks Father Seraphin used. We hear no further mention of Charles having difficulties with his studies. He would never be a great theologian like Blessed Dominic, but he was able to deal with the material put before him as a student. Besides, he had other gifts in abundance, more important in a religious than intellectual ability, as one of his classmates recalled:

He was an example of devotion, full of faith and piety, strict in keeping our rules, simple and friendly to live with. His tender and honest nature, his artless all-embracing piety, his good humour and natural cheerfulness during recreation made everyone love and respect him.

Another description of Charles as a student was given by Brother Anthony Raaymakers:

He was an excellent religious, with the gentleness of an angel. You could have knocked him over and, instead of a complaint, you would have got only a lovely, gentle smile. He was always content with a little and took everything in good part. If he happened to neglect any of his duties, he would always apologise or acknowledge his fault in public.

Although not yet ordained, Charles was shaping up to be just the kind of person Blessed Dominic wanted for the English foundation. Writing to the Superior General to ask him to send another priest to England, Dominic had said,

It does not matter whether he has great talent or not. What does matter is that he should have plenty of good will, and be prepared to suffer many things – derision, mockery and contempt. That would, to a great extent, be his lot here. Those who come must not look for comforts, but a full meal of insult and outrage of every kind.

Dominic was speaking here from bitter experience. He had arrived in England only twelve years after Catholic Emancipation and there was still a great deal of suspicion and even hatred of Catholicism to be encountered. Every Sunday morning as he walked the two miles from the monastery at Aston to the town of Stone to celebrate Mass, Dominic would be insulted and attacked. As an eye-witness recalled:

Behind him surged a rabble of all the local wastrels, from whose mouths came words of ribald and unrepeatable insult. As he passed under the windows the more respectable citizens joined in the hideous outcry against the Demon, the Papist, the Devil! Slowly then in the midst of his horrible escort walked Father Dominic, aflame with love for souls. Stones and mud rained upon him. Once, at a later time, he was asked how he had got the terrible scar on his forehead. It was, as he at last confessed, caused by a violent blow from a stone used as a weapon.

This was the missionary life for which the young religious were being prepared. From Blessed Dominic, Charles and his fellow-students would have heard of the work that was to be done in England, a work of reconciliation. They would also have heard something of the sufferings they might expect to find there, sufferings which, as Dominic admitted in a letter to a friend, he found extremely painful:

I spent so many years before coming to this Island preparing myself, at all times, for suffering. And now, it seems to me that, if I had ever foreseen all that awaited me, I should never have had the courage to step on board ship. Such sufferings, and of every kind, too, would be too much for a giant. Last Sunday I broke down and wept bitterly. I can do no more. The cross is too heavy. My God! if you intend to increase it, you must increase my strength, too.

Blessed Dominic visited Ere for the last time in July 1849. At the end of his visit, when he was leaving to return to England, the students, among whom was Charles, were reluctant to let him go. As one of them recalled:

The students, of whom I was one, obtained permission to go with him to Tournai. When we were about a quarter of an hour's walk from the town Father Dominic stopped and said: 'My sons, you may go back now. Embrace me – it is the last time in this world. But I hope one day to embrace you again in heaven'. We remarked that he was young still, and in good health, and that there was no reason to speak like that. 'I tell you', he replied, 'it is the last time – good-bye'.

A month later he lay dying on the platform of Pangbourne railway station.

On Saturday, 21 December 1850, Charles was ordained to the priesthood by Monsignor Gaspare Labis, Bishop of Tournai. The ceremony took place in the Bishop's Chapel, beside the Cathedral. Charles had been ordained deacon on 25 May and now at the end of the year he became a priest. 1850 was a very happy year for him, but it was also a year of great sorrow, four months before his ordination, on 7 August, his father had died. It must have saddened Charles, as he celebrated Mass for the first time, to think that his father had not lived to see him ordained and to receive his first blessing. In fact, none of his family was present at the ordination; his only link with home was the companion of his schooldays, Michael Emons, who was ordained with Charles.

Peter Joseph Houben, Charles' younger brother, had in the meantime entered the diocesan seminary and was studying for the priesthood. In a letter written to Charles on 21 September 1851, Peter talks about how he had intended to visit Ere, but was advised to change his plans:

I really intended visiting you during the vacation, but unfortunately I had to renounce my purpose with regret. As my brothers and sisters wished also to go to Ere they advised me to put off this agreeable journey to a more favourable time.... Time destroys monuments, but your memory will never be erased from our hearts.... Father Ignatius Spencer has been preaching a holy crusade in the seminaries, asking prayers for England's conversion. He left our

College for Germany and was received with marks of distinction in Cologne by his Eminence the Cardinal, who offered him a house as a foundation of the Congregation of the Passion.

Unfortunately, the favourable time for Charles' brothers and sisters to visit him did not come; on 16 February 1852 he left Holy Cross Retreat, Ere. The Provincial, Father Eugene Martorelli, had called him to England.

III

Learning a Little English

On the first stage of his journey Charles was accompanied by one of the community of Holy Cross Retreat; Father Turrenius, an Italian Passionist who had worked in England before coming to Ere travelled with him as far as Dover. In a letter written to his family on 2 March 1852 Charles describes what happened after he left Belgium:

My journey from Belgium to England went very well. A priest from Belgium accompanied me as far as Dover and after this I travelled alone, for the most part by train. At times I travelled along under the ground and so I found myself in complete darkness. Everything went quite well during the sailing; I did, in fact, feel a little uncomfortable, but the fact that it was raining and was quite windy has to be taken into account, and soon after the crossing I recovered completely. We have a monastery near London and I stayed there for two days. From there I left for Aston Hall, staying five days in that house. I then headed for Saint Wilfrid's with our Rev. Father Provincial, and it is in this beautiful monastery that I am to stay. I have already grown used to the English climate and am beginning to speak a little English; pray for me that I learn to speak the language like a true Englishman, and pray also for the poor Protestants of England that one day they will be converted to the true faith. I pray often for you all.

The monastery near London in which Charles stayed for two days was at Kilburn. This house, known as the Hyde, in Cool Oak Lane (otherwise known as Wood Lane), was the London home of the Passionists before the opening of Saint Joseph's Retreat, Highgate. Saint Michael's Retreat, Aston Hall, where Charles spent five days after leaving the Hyde, was near the town of Stone in Staffordshire. Founded by Blessed Dominic Barberi ten years earlier, it was the first Passionist house in England. Charles' final destination, Saint Wilfrid's Retreat, Cotton Hall, was also in Staffordshire, but further north, near Cheadle.

After his conversion to Catholicism in 1845, Frederick William Faber had founded a religious community which he called the Company of the Will of God. Lord Shrewsbury, a Catholic, gave Faber a house across the valley from his own home, Alton Towers. This house, Cotton Hall, became the home of Faber's community who during their short lifespan were also known as the Wilfridians. When in 1848 Newman returned from Rome to introduce the Oratorians, Faber, who was then thirty-four, decided that the will of God was that he and his companions should transfer to the Oratory. Saint Wilfrid's was offered by Faber to the Passionists, who made it their House of Studies.

In bringing Charles to Saint Wilfrid's the Provincial hoped that he would have a better opportunity of learning English well. At that time many of the priests in the English Passionist monasteries were Italian; here at Saint Wilfrid's, living with the English and Irish students, Charles could begin to speak a little English.

About a month after Charles' arrival the community were visited by Father Ignatius Spencer. A former Anglican clergyman and son of Lord Spencer, Father Ignatius had been the first non-Italian Passionist to hold the office of Provincial, having been nominated by Blessed Dominic as his successor. Dominic had held Ignatius in the highest esteem and had written of him to Father Pius Cayro, one of his former students, 'If you could only see what a splendid man he is! What zeal, what ardour for the glory of God! He seems like a new Saint Paul'.

Father Ignatius already knew Charles from Belgium, and he had also been introduced to his brother Peter Joseph when he visited the seminary to ask for prayers for England. In fact, he had met the other members of Charles' family, including his father, when on 28 August 1849 he had visited Munstergeleen with Brother Anthony Raaymakers. For Charles' family this may have been the first opportunity of seeing the Passionist habit, as we learn from a letter Ignatius wrote a week after leaving Munstergeleen, in which he describes how he was travelling:

I came first to Ere and started on my journey from thence, being joined by one of the lay brothers from that house, called Brother

Anthony, a Dutchman, at Brussells, and with him I am travelling thro' Holland in our habits more in the style of monks than I have found myself before but this does not mean much discomfort.

Ignatius, who could speak French, Italian and German, had started learning Dutch two years before his visit to Munstergeleen and so would have been able to converse with Charles' family. Meeting Charles again in Cotton Hall, he would have been able to note how he was settling into life in his new home. In a letter written to the Provincial, Father Eugene, on 24 April 1852, a week after his visit to Saint Wilfrid's, Ignatius, who was then First Provincial Consultor, gives evidence of the good impression Charles made on him and refers to him as someone who could be relied upon to maintain a sense of order and act responsibly.

In June 1852 a new student arrived at Saint Wilfrid's from the novitiate. His name was Paul Mary Pakenham. A son of the Earl of Longford and nephew of the Duke of Wellington, he had been a Catholic for only two years. He was three months older than Charles and had been a captain in the Grenadier Guards before becoming a Passionist. Born in Dublin, it was he who would be chosen four years later as superior of the first Passionist house in Ireland, Mount Argus. No doubt these two young men, both ex-soldiers but from different armies and with very different backgrounds, felt drawn to each other by the generous spirit which each recognised in the other. As they talked to each other in the gardens of Cotton Hall, Paul Mary helping Charles with his English lessons, little did they think that one day both their names would be linked with an Irish monastery, founded by one and sanctified by the other.

A year after his arrival in England, Charles was transferred to Saint Michael's Retreat, Aston Hall, arriving there on 5 February. There were six others in the community: three priests, all of whom were Italian, and three brothers, of whom two were Dutch and one, Brother Michael Behan, Irish. Brother Michael was to spend many years with Charles, first in England and later in Ireland.

Unlike Saint Wilfrid's, where there were few Catholics, Saint Michael's Parish was growing rapidly. Located in an area which was more industrial than rural, it had become home for many of the Irish immigrants who had poured into England as a result of the famine of 1846. Assigned to work in the parish, Charles found himself ministering often to people who were exiles, as he was. He felt drawn to the 'poor Irish' who seemed to him very like his own people. At the same time he did not forget that he had been sent to work for the people of England, as can be seen from a letter he wrote to his family on 16 September 1853 in which he says,

Pray for the Protestants of England and Holland, that God may grant them the grace of a sincere conversion. Our blessed founder, Father Paul of the Cross, prayed for fifty years for the conversion of England.

Charles' first experience of parish work lasted less than two years. On 13 October 1854 the novitiate was transferred from

Saint Saviour's Retreat, Broadway, Worcestershire to Saint Wilfrid's, Cotton Hall, and about a month later Charles was sent to Saint Wilfrid's as assistant to the Novice Master, Father Salvian Nardocci.

Father Salvian was a remarkable man in many ways. A great lover of order, he held the office of Master of Novices for many years. In every house in which he lived we find him making a catalogue of the books in the library, arranging the music in the church, repairing the vestments and tidying the sacristy, finding a place for everything and putting everything in its place. He drew up the liturgical calendar for the Province each year. Any references to the Passionists in the newspapers he would cut out and paste into his books of cuttings. He had a great sense of history and was a compulsive writer, not of letters but of what we might as a general term call 'memories': biographies, historical records and, most important for our purposes, a diary. This diary, covering a period of about thirty years, is one of our most valuable sources of information about Charles.

Not many months after his arrival at Saint Wilfrid's, Father Salvian was given other duties which kept him away from the novitiate for quite a while. In one of the neighbouring parishes, about seven miles from Cotton Hall, lived a parish priest who quite literally thought he owned the church. This man was under the mistaken impression that the late Earl of Shrewsbury, who had built the church and presbytery, had left both buildings to him in his will. Consequently, when Bishop Ullathorne tried to transfer him to another parish, he refused to go, saying, according to Salvian, that no one, not even the Bishop, could remove him from that place. The Bishop, wishing to avoid any publicity, sent the Vicar General to visit him, to try to settle the matter quietly. Salvian tells us that the Vicar General tried everything to induce the Priest to obey the Bishop, but all in vain. Seeing that he was making no progress,

he went into the Sexton's house, to ask for the key of the church, which was kept by him. The Parish Priest followed a few minutes after, and entering the house, without much ceremony, took the poor Vicar General by the collar and thrust him out of the house, into the public street. Several people saw the poor Vicar General treated by the priest as above. In a few minutes the whole village came to know about what had happened, and it naturally gave great scandal. As soon as the Vicar General had freed himself from the grasp of the Parish Priest, there and then, in the public street and in the presence of several people who happened to be there, he suspended him as he justly deserved.

The next day Bishop Ullathorne wrote to Saint Wilfrid's, asking the superior to appoint a priest to look after the parish in question until the situation would be resolved. Father Saivian was sent and over a long period of time succeeded not only in caring for the parish but also in reconciling the parish priest and his Bishop. Salvian was fortunate in having Charles as Vice Master at this time, as it meant he could be away from Saint Wilfrid's without anxiety, as he himself realised when he wrote: 'As Father Charles took great care of the novices, I let him have the whole care of them, except that I heard their confessions, and conferences'.

In the Central Archives of the Passionists in England is a book on the front of which is written *Book of the General Administration of Saint Wilfrid's Retreat*; it is a book which tells a sad story in few words:

February 1855. From the accounts made with Father Vicar results that remains in hand from last month seven shillings.
March 1855. In Father Vicar's hand nothing.
April 1855. In Father Vicar's hand one pound, three shillings and ninepence.
May 1855. We find that Father Vicar has spent the money which was in his hands.
June 1855. Father Vicar has spent all the money which was in his hands.

Although the parish attached to Saint Wilfrid's was 'immensely large in extent of territory', there were only a handful of Catholics and these were not able to provide for the needs of the religious community and its novices. The late Earl had wanted a monastery near at hand and had been a generous support to the community but his successor, who was not a Catholic, could hardly be expected to show the same interest. Father Salvian explains the situation and its outcome:

During the summer Saint Wilfrid's was something like a terrestrial paradise, but in winter the cold and damp were insupportable. We were very poor, and had no means to keep up fires in our rooms.... Novices also were not coming, and those few who came, besides not having brought anything, finding the place too cold and damp in winter, left us one after the other, except one. There was no alternative but to starve or leave the place. We decided on the latter.

On 8 November 1855 Father Salvian returned to Broadway, taking with him his one remaining novice. Most of the other members of the community also went to their new homes. Charles and another priest, Father Raymond Disano, stayed on at Saint Wilfrid's until a diocesan priest would be sent to care for the parish. Although his parishioners were scattered over a wide area and his appointment was only a temporary one, Charles set about visiting the homes of the people with his usual determination. However, three months later the new parish priest arrived and the two Passionists moved on, Father Raymond to Broadway and Charles to Saint Anne's Retreat, Sutton.

It would be difficult to imagine two more different settings for a monastery than Cotton and Sutton, the first situated in a remote corner of the English countryside, the other in the busy Lancashire town of Saint Helens. Describing the monastery to which he had just been sent, Charles writes, in a letter to his uncle:

It is beside the railway, and there are lots of factories nearby, including a fine, big glassworks. We are not far from the cities of Manchester and Liverpool.

Charles was there for only a few months, but this was just his introduction to Sutton; he would return later and would spend five years working as a curate in Saint Anne's Parish.

On 25 June he was transferred to London. What he did there we cannot say; no mention of him is made in any of the records of the London community from that time. Four weeks after Charles' arrival at the Hyde, Father Paul Mary Pakenham came to London from Rome. He was on his way to Dublin where he was to be the first Rector of the new foundation at Mount Argus. No doubt he and Charles were delighted to see one another again. They did not realise that thev would never meet again; within twelve months Charles would be trans- ferred to Dublin, but Paul Mary would be dead.

IV

Mount Argus

On the feast of Mary, Mother of Holy Hope, 9 July 1857, Charles set foot for the first time on Irish soil. The 'Island of Saints and Scholars' was to be his home for a total of almost thirty years and his final resting-place. However that was still a long way off; he was now only thirty-five years old and had been a priest for less than five years.

The red-brick house known as Mount Argus, on the outskirts of Dublin, had been taken by the Passionists on 15 August 1856. Less than eight months later the new community had experienced a sharing in the Cross with the death of their young rector, Father Paul Mary Pakenham. His successor, Father Osmund Maguire, arrived to find a group of men who were discouraged, overworked and suffering from malnutrition. It was obvious that an injection of life was needed; he asked the Provincial and Charles was sent.

The new arrival lost no time in settling in and taking more

than his share of the work. Charles had already worked with the Irish immigrants in England and had been drawn to them, finding them very like his own people. In a letter written to his uncle not long after his arrival at Mount Argus he says,

I came to Dublin, the capital of Ireland, on 9 July 1857. The people here speak English. Our congregation has only one house in Ireland; here we have five Passionist priests and five lay-brothers. In spite of the large number of Catholics in Ireland, there are very few priests and I have to say two masses every Sunday. We have to hear confessions from morning till night nearly every day. If we had twelve priests here, they would all be kept busy preaching and hearing confessions. Much good can be done here in the Lord's vineyard. As you know, Ireland is a Catholic country.... For more than three hundred years the Irish have been cruelly persecuted but have remained loyal to the Catholic faith in spite of everything.

For Charles and for all the community the early years at Mount Argus were demanding. However, Father Osmund's mind was on the future. The farmhouse in which the ten religious were leading their cramped existence, described by the chronicler as looking like a slice cut from a factory, was far too small to meet the needs of a growing community; it would have to go! Always one for thinking big, Father Osmund engaged J. J. Mc-Carthy, the foremost architect of nineteenth-century Ireland, to design a monastery which could accommodate the religious community, provide additional cells and classrooms for students and incorporate a retreat centre for laymen, the first of its kind in Ireland. McCarthy submitted a design in Romanesque style for a building with about eighty rooms, to be constructed in Wicklow granite. The design was accepted by the community and on 13 June the foundation-stone was laid by the auxiliary bishop, Dr Whelan, 'thousands of the Catholic body having congregated in the charming grounds attached to the Retreat', according to the Evening News. In solving one problem Father Osmund was creating another: large monasteries have to be paid for. So it was that Charles was given a task which, though seldom referred to, was to occupy him from time to time for many years, that is, collecting money to pay for the building of Mount Argus. With Brother Michael Behan as his companion, he went questing all over Ireland, to places as far apart as Kerry and Tyrone. His simplicity and compassion made him welcome wherever he went, receiving from others but also giving advice and comfort, turning his work of collecting into a valuable apostolate. He was always grateful to those who helped; at the same time, he was not blind or insensitive to what was going on around him, as we see in a letter to his brother, Father Peter Joseph Houben.

Here in Dublin we have built a huge monastery which cost about eight thousand pounds. The Irish gave us this money; they are very generous when it comes to their Catholic faith. However, here in the city of Dublin and in the surrounding districts there are also thousands of people who neither go to confession nor make their Easter communion. With all my heart I implore you to pray for them, to offer your evening Rosary for the conversion of so many great sinners; go to mass and offer your communions for this intention. I shudder when I think of how often our Lord is offended in this large city, crucified by serious sins. Ah, pray that these sinners may turn back to God.

The Passionist rule, written by Saint Paul of the Cross, with its emphasis on poverty and penance, solitude and constant prayer, has as its aim the formation of a certain kind of person: an 'apostolic mystic'. In an account of the Congregation written in 1747, Saint Paul says of the Passionists,

Their life is like that of the Apostles; even more, it is totally conformed to these and the apostles' conduct is the norm for the Constitutions which endeavour to form a man totally God-centred, totally apostolic, a man of prayer, detached from the world, from things, from himself so that he may in all truth be called a disciple of Jesus Christ.

Charles was well aware that his effectiveness as a priest was indissolubly linked to his commitment to a life of prayer. Before his brother Peter's ordination, he had written to him, 'the more you prepare yourself, the greater will be the graces you receive from God'. During these first years in Dublin the Holy Spirit was to lead him into another ministry, the one for which he is most remembered today. Father Sebastian Keens has left us this account of an early incident in which the healing power of God was shown through the prayer and blessing of Father Charles of Mount Argus:

A boy about twelve years of age, having lost the use of his legs, was brought to me by his mother. I made no delay in calling Father Charles to bless him. Whilst Father Charles was blessing the boy, I put on my secular dress to go into Dublin. Great, indeed, was my surprise to find the little fellow walking in front of the house waiting for me, perfectly cured.

Other cures followed and soon people were coming to Mount Argus not just to be blessed but to be blessed by Father Charles; those who were too ill to travel to the monastery would send for him. Joseph Moore, a witness at the Apostolic Processes, gives this testimony:

I heard from my mother of a striking instance which happened about 1861. Father Charles had been called to visit a granduncle of mine, Thomas Doyle. He resided at 23 Lower Ormonde Quay. Father Charles came, saw the sick man and, when about to leave, surprised the members of the family by saying 'There is another sick person here': they had not told him that a daughter of the sick man, Johanna Teresa, was actually very ill with fever. They were not prepared to bring a visitor as the room had not been duly tidied up, and tried to dissuade Father Charles from going to see her. He however insisted on doing so. My mother always emphasised that nobody had told Father Charles about the sick girl....

She was suffering from typhus fever or some virulent fever, and was so reduced that the doctor [Dr Willis] said that unless she got immediate rest and sleep she would die. She had not slept for some days before that. When Father Charles came in, she was sitting up in bed raving in delirium. She was at the crisis of her fever and had been refusing to take the prescribed remedies. He gently put his hand on her forehead and pushed her down to a lying posture. She almost at once went to sleep and when the doctor returned next morning, the crisis was passed and he pronounced her out of danger. My mother often spoke of this matter and said she considered it a miracle. The doctor, I was told, also looked on it as miraculous.

In this case, not only do we see the Holy Spirit working through Charles with the gift of healing, but we also observe how the Spirit enlightened him, making him aware of the presence of the second sick person in the house. What exactly was Charles' own reaction to events such as these we cannot say; he never spoke about any of the cures. Certainly it must have tested his faith in the power of God when sick people would come and ask to be blessed. On one occasion a man whose child was sick said to him, 'You must cure my child', to which, we are told, Charles replied, 'There is no "must" with God'. Obviously he was only too aware that the cures which took place were not the result of any powers which he possessed, but had as their source the kindness and mercy of God.

On 8 September 1863 the new Retreat of Blessed Paul of the Cross, Mount Argus was blessed by Archbishop Cullen of Dublin. (Saint Paul of the Cross was not canonised until 1867.) A newspaper report described it as 'the noblest religious house erected in these countries since the Reformation.... The whole exterior is built of granite, and although of the greatest plainness of character and simplicity of design, as is required by the spirit of the Order, yet from its height, massiveness, and boldness of outline, it produces quite a monastic effect'. The community continued to use the small temporary church which had been built onto the original farmhouse. Plans for a new church had been made, but as yet it was not possible to proceed. Archbishop Cullen was opposed to the project as he believed there was no need for a large church so far from the centre of the city. However, the people were undeterred by the distance and were now coming in large numbers to be blessed by Charles, with unfortunate consequences for him:

For some time his health had been very much impaired, in consequence of his constantly attending the people, coming from every part of Ireland, and some from England, Scotland, and even from America for his blessing. It is said that many were cured from their maladies, but we never took any step to have the 'miracles', as the people called them, verified. Every hour of the day, from morning till evening, people were coming for Father Charles' blessing and miracle. The poor saintly man had not a moment's rest. Day by day, he was getting weaker and weaker.

– Annals of the Anglo-Hibernian Province

In his diary Father Salvian writes that at this time 'the poor man [Charles] had not a moment to himself. The consequence was that he got very thin and weak, for not taking care of himself'. The superiors considered moving him to another house for the sake of his health. However, before they reached their decision, something happened which compelled them to remove Charles from Dublin.

Amongst the sick, lame, blind, deaf, etc. several beggars intruded themselves, soliciting alms; and some others filled up bottles and jars with Holy Water, which every day was blessed by Father Charles, and sold it to simple people, not only in the City of Dublin, but in other cities and towns. This simoniacal dealing of those wretched devotees came to the ear of the Archbishop of Dublin, Dr Cullen, who advised our superiors to remove for some time Father Charles from Dublin, and that would be the only remedy to put a stop to the scandalous dealing of those persons. The superiors were very glad for the suggestion of his Grace, and sent Father Charles to England.

– Annals

Father Salvian writes in his diary, 'Of course the poor man never dreamed that people would do such a thing, and make their fortune by selling Holy Water; he was ignorant of it all along'. The fact that he stresses the point of Charles' innocence only makes it more clear that Charles was indeed under suspicion of being involved. He tells us that the selling of the blessed water was the Archbishop's 'principal reason' for asking the Provincial to remove Charles. There had also been some adverse publicity, in the form of a letter to *Saunders' Newsletter*, a newspaper well known for its hostility to the Catholic Church:

Sir,

I have the honour to be attached as Medical Officer to one of the hospitals of this city. A few days ago a poor girl having both her eyes destroyed by purulent ophthalmia applied at the hospital for advice. I asked her why she had not sought medical aid sooner, informing her at the same time that her case was now hopeless. She made the following extraordinary statement. About six weeks previously one of her eyes became inflamed and, as she did not derive any benefit from remedies she had been advised to try, she applied to the Blessed(!) Fathers of Harold's Cross [Mount Argus]. These gentlemen rubbed her eyes with 'the relics', ordered her to take holy water internally, and told her not to go near the doctors. She remained under this treatment until both her eyes were destroyed.

Thus, a poor girl, who under proper medical treatment could have been perfectly cured of her disease, is now thrown into the poorhouse by those who, under the mask of religion, have done their utmost to ruin her not only in this world, but in that which is to come.

Medicus.

Obviously the letter was directed against Charles. Whatever the source of the accusations may have been, there is no doubt that Charles never discouraged anyone from seeking medical attention. On the contrary he had the greatest respect for doctors; in her testimony at the Apostolic Processes, Elizabeth Nally states, 'My mother used to tell me that she once brought an elder sister of mine, who had a swelling under her ear, to Father Charles. He told her to bring the child to a doctor because God in his goodness had given doctors skill to heal'.

Nevertheless, in spite of his innocence in both cases, to England he was sent. His being removed after these occurrences might have seemed to others to imply his guilt, but nothing was said. His new home was to be the novitiate house, Saint Saviour's Retreat, Broadway, where he would be sure to have the rest he needed. On the evening of 3 July 1866 Charles slipped away from Mount Argus. His friend, Brother Michael came with him to the boat, to help with his luggage and to wave goodbye.

V

Quiet and Hidden

Charles had set out from Mount Argus anticipating a long and lonely journey to Saint Saviour's. Things turned out differently, however, as one of the novices noted in the Novitiate Chronicles:

Wednesday, 4 July 1866.
Today the Rev. Father Charles arrived from Dublin and also Brother Michael, a lay Brother, came with him by mistake. According to his own story he was intent on arranging the berth of Father Charles when the boat put out to sea and so he thought he would come all the way and make a good job of a bad one.

Brother Michael was rewarded for his mistake with a few days' holiday in Broadway, staying until 9 July, when the farewell was repeated in reverse, with Charles accompanying him as far as Evesham.

Although Charles had never been stationed in Broadway before, there were some familiar faces among the community.

The Novice Master was Father Raymond Disano, who had worked with him in Saint Wilfrid's Parish, Cotton and, subsequently, at Mount Argus. Father Raymond knew that he had been sent to Saint Saviour's to rest and so he took him under his wing; by bringing him for walks in the country and inviting him to the novices' recreation he helped Charles to relax after the strain of recent events in Dublin and, slowly, to rebuild his strength.

After a while Charles was able to take part in some of the works of the community. His voice was put to good use in the liturgy: we find him singing the Gospel at the High Mass on Sundays and the lessons at Matins on feast days. There was a small parish attached to the monastery and occasionally he would help the Parish Priest, but always under the watchful eye of Father Raymond.

Charles stayed at Broadway about a year and a half; it was for him like a second novitiate experience. His room was near the chapel and he took advantage of the peace and quiet of the house, devoting more time to prayer than had been possible in Dublin. On 27 November 1867 the Provincial, seeing that his state of health was greatly improved and that he would now be ready for something more demanding, transferred Charles to Saint Anne's Retreat, Sutton. The novices were sorry to see him go, but glad to have had the opportunity of getting to know him, as we read in the Novitiate Chronicles:

His departure was like his whole life, quiet, and hidden for the sake of Him, for whom alone he lives. He did not, however, go without taking an affectionate farewell of all. He visited the novices in the recreation room, and after taking his leave of each one separately, and giving him his blessing, he left, expressing a wish 'to see them all again before he'd die'. May we all follow the example he left us!

'This evening arrived here from Broadway Father Charles who is appointed to remain here as a member of this community', noted the Rector of Saint Anne's Retreat in his diary; with these words Father Salvian Nardocci, now in Sutton, began once more to record for us Charles' activities. Father Salvian had handed over the care of the Novitiate to Father Raymond the previous year, moving to Sutton as Rector and Parish Priest. His task was not an easy one as the parish was very large but, he tells us,

I was fortunate in having a very good community of religious, always ready for any work according to their condition: the priests in preaching, hearing confessions, attending sick-calls, going for supplies, or preaching Charity Sermons, and every other sacred duty of our ministry, and the lay-brothers in performing their special duties cheerfully, and carefully, so that I had no occasion of complaining of any one. I do not mean that we were all saints, but I say only that I had good subjects who did their duty to my satisfaction and, I hope, to their merit.

Charles was a valuable addition to the community, and Father Salvian put him to work immediately, visiting the sick and burying the dead, instructing in the school and preaching in the church. In his sermons, which were very simple, it was his sincerity which touched the hearts of those who heard him, as we learn from Father Cyprian Meagher:

When I was a student in Lancashire I was told by my brethren that when he was in that place some time before, he was preaching on one occasion on the Eternal Truths and was so overcome by the realisation of what he was saying that he could not continue and had to be brought down weeping.

At Cotton Hall Father Salvian had given Charles the 'whole care' of the novices. Now at Sutton the same thing was happening, as he began to put Charles' generosity to good use. According to Father Salvian,

Night and day, he was called to the sick: he administered the Holy Sacraments, remained until a late hour in the confessional, catechised, preached: in a word, the burden of the work fell upon the shoulders of Father Charles.

While at Sutton, however, Charles' ministry was not confined to his own parish. We read of him being sent to help in other places, such as Warrington, Widnes and even, from time to time, Mount Argus. Nor were his contacts with Ireland confined to these visits. He received frequent letters asking for his prayers and occasionally a visitor would arrive from Ireland to ask for his blessing; Father Salvian notes on 1 April 1868 that 'a poor sickly young man came here from Dublin to be blessed by Father Charles. He left Sutton this afternoon'.

On 25 September 1872, after almost five years at Saint Anne's Retreat, Charles was moved to London, to Saint Joseph's Retreat, Highgate. This time he stayed fifteen months in London but, as before, there is no information to be found about what he did there; the house records tell us only the date of his arrival at Highgate and the date on which he left.

VI

Extraordinary Cures

Saturday. This morning arrived here Father Charles Houben from Highgate, London, being appointed for this community. Father Charles is well
known in this city of Dublin as well as throughout Ireland for the many
miraculous cures people say [they] have received by his blessing them with
the relic of Saint Paul [of the Cross], and by using Holy Water blessed
with the same relic. Father Charles was one of the first Fathers who came
to Dublin after its foundation in 1856 and had left in 1867, when he was
removed from Dublin for the reason of his having become too remarkable
for extraordinary cures.

This entry in the diary of Father Salvian records for us the return of Charles to Mount Argus on 10 January 1874. The news
of his arrival spread quickly and, within a short time, the daily
pilgrimages of sick and suffering had begun once more. The
people of Ireland had not forgotten him during his eight years
of exile; they remembered Charles as someone who always
had time to listen to their troubles, one who was always ready
to comfort those in need and show them the goodness and
loving kindness of God our Saviour.

In the Ordinary and Apostolic Processes, the two most

striking aspects of Charles' life, referred to again and again, both in the evidence of his fellow Passionists and in that of people who had sought his help, are that he was always available to those in any kind or suffering and that he lived continually in the presence of God. In its Document on the Ministry and Life of Priests, *Presbyterorum Ordinis*, the Second Vatican Council affirmed that priests 'cannot be ministers of Christ unless they are witnesses and dispensers of a life other than this earthly one. But', the document goes on to say, 'they cannot be of service to people if they remain strangers to the life and conditions of men and women' (Chap. 3). Charles is a clear example of someone who witnessed to spiritual values by a life of prayer and, at the same time, was completely involved in the day-to-day reality of the lives of the men and women of his time.

In a letter to his brothers and sisters, written from Mount Argus, Charles says, 'My duties in the monastery are as follows: I say Mass every day; I preach and hear confessions; I say prayers and bless the people who come to the church'. As always, he says nothing about the cures which were taking place. For information about these we must turn to others. A Dublin businessman, John Patterson, tells his story:

I saw Father Charles when I was about six or seven years of age. That was in the year 1876. I was stone-blind as the result of an accident which occurred when I was nearly four-and-a-half. I was hammering a rock of some kind and a lot of chips flew off and struck both eyes. I had perfect vision before this and was at school. I was at least eighteen months blind. I was brought to two or three oculists who treated my eyes, perhaps by drops. At any rate, I know that the treatment was painful. I do not know what was the supervening cause of the blindness; and there is no person now living who could give information on this point. I suppose I could have distinguished day from night during these eighteen months, but I could not see anything. My step-mother and father often referred to the fact that I was blind during this period. Members of the family and strangers were also convinced on this point. Some lady whom I don't know told my stepmother who was a Protestant to have me brought to Father Charles. This lady brought me to Mount Argus. I came in a cab, and was led into the church. I could see nobody, and I thought I was alone in the church. I was brought to the altar-rails. All I remember clearly is that in a moment I saw Father Charles with his hands extended horizontally towards my eyes. I did not hear him speaking, and I do not know whether he touched my eyes or raised my eyelids or not. I then left the church but I don't remember having seen anything on the way out. When I was leaving the grounds of Mount Argus, I looked to my right hand side and saw a cow. I cried out, 'Oh! Look at the cow'. The cow appeared to me to be very small: and the field seemed to be in a hollow, whereas it was really level. The lady who accompanied me was surprised and said that it was a cow. I am sure it was the same evening that I saw all the members of the family. I remember that there was excitement in the house at my return.

Once again Charles' ministry was not confined to those who came to see him at Mount Argus; day and night, he was ready to visit the sick in their homes or in hospitals.

On the occasion of Father Charles' visit to the house of which I will speak, a great crowd had assembled in anticipation of his coming, and even a Protestant woman asked him to come and bless her child, which he did.

I believe Father Charles worked a miracle in the case of my uncle. It was in the year 1878, or thereabouts, when my uncle was thirty-two, and I about fourteen. I lived in the same room with this man. I have a perfectly clear memory of what happened. One morning my uncle did not come to work as usual, and word was brought that he was spitting blood. I never heard that he had spat blood previously. The doctor – a famous Dr Hamilton – came to see him and said that he could not live beyond that night. The doctor applied no remedies, contenting himself with advising my uncle to set his affairs in order and send for the priest. I don't remember having heard the doctor say where the haemorrhage was. The haemorrhage was very copious. He vomited more blood than one would think the body could contain. My uncle's wife suggested that Father Charles should be sent for. The sick man had received the last sacraments. He was very weak and could not stir when Father Charles came in the afternoon. He was conscious. I was in the house at the time, but was not present at the interview between Father Charles and the sick man. Father Charles came into the room in which we were assembled awaiting results and said that the man would be all right. This put our minds at ease as we had great trust in Father Charles. Father Charles said he would visit him again, and so he did, after about two days. Immediately after Father Charles' first visit the haemorrhage stopped and was better in every way. My uncle remained in bed until after Father Charles' second visit. After Father Charles' second visit he got up and went out, and carried on his business as well as ever. The doctor came again shortly after Father Charles' visit and expressed astonishment to the Keogh family that the man was alive and well. The doctor had no further trouble with him. He never got a haemorrhage again, and died as the result of contracting a cold in 1885.

The 'great crowd assembled in anticipation of his coming',

described above by John Hendrick, is reminiscent of a scene from the Gospel or the Acts of the Apostles. So great was people's confidence in his prayers and his blessing that large numbers would gather outside any house he visited and, even as he went along the street, sick people would be brought out of their homes to be blessed by him.

When I was a very small baby, about three or four months old, my uncle let me fall. I developed spinal disease. I was bent double, my head bent back and my hands resting on my knees when I tried to walk, on crutches till nine years. One day (we lived then in Mercer Street) my mother happened to bring me out of the house when Father Charles was passing. He asked who I was and what was wrong. My mother told him and he blessed me and told me to say one Our Father and three Hail Marys each morning and night in honour of the Passion. In about two or three months I could walk straight, my head in normal position, and my hands and arms also normal. During the two months the improvement was gradual and I have remained in good health ever since.

In spite of the constant demands being made on his time, Charles never gave the impression of being someone who was caught up in a whirlwind of activity. On the contrary, even while engaged in his ministry he seemed to be totally absorbed in God:

I knew Father Charles personally from about 1869 when I was a schoolboy. I often saw him and spoke to him from that until he died.... I am sure Father Charles was a man of uncommon holiness. I recollect especially his attitude which clearly showed that he was absorbed in prayer and oblivious of his worldly surroundings: he always had a prayer book or crucifix in his hand. I remember well the wonderful smile which radiated from his countenance when I saw him speaking words of comfort to a poor boy who was suffering: he seemed transformed and even handsome, though normally he was by no means good-looking.

Elizabeth Costello, who testified at the Apostolic Processes, was the daughter of John Smyth, a Dublin cab-driver, who often was sent to Mount Argus to bring Charles to the sick and the dying:

My father was a cab proprietor and very frequently drove Father Charles on his visits to the sick. In this ministry Father Charles was most devoted and responded most readily to all calls.

... When being driven about to the sick, he would be entirely absorbed in prayer and quite unconscious of his surroundings. He would have to be called when arrived at his destination. My father told me that Father Charles was always praying. When going to the sick in his cab, Father Charles prayed all the time: if it was dark, he had to be given a candle to read by. On arrival at the end of his journey, he would be so absorbed in prayer that he would have to be called.

Sometimes my father had to accompany him twice in the same day on his rounds or visits. These visits were made in all weathers and at all times, often late at night. Father Charles seemed to respond immediately to any call upon his charitable ministry.

Before blessing a sick person he would usually pray spontaneously for some time; often too he would write out prayers for those who came to see him, prayers which were always simple and adapted to those who would use them. Here is one, given to a little girl in June 1877 for her First Communion:

Sweetest Mother of God, lend me your heart to place the little infant Jesus on it. Praise, adore and love Him for me, as you can do it so much better than I. Amen.

When Saint Paul's Retreat had been opened in 1863 the community had been unable to proceed with the building of the church. The original drawing of the monastery-to-be, by McCarthy, had included at the east end of the building a church with an enormous spire, more neo-Gothic than Romanesque in inspiration. Fortunately, when in the 1870s work began on the new church, the plans for this building could not be found. McCarthy now came up with a better idea: a Romanesque facade with twin towers, which would blend much better with the monastery and give us Mount Argus as we know it today.

James Burke was in his early twenties when work began on the church:

I knew Father Charles from the year when the new church was started here, about sixty years ago. He was the talk of the whole district.... I came here to work on the new church and shortly afterwards he called me aside and said to me, 'There was an accident here already to one of the workmen: tell the others not to be afraid; there will be no other accident'.

He was always praying: you could see his lips moving in prayer. He went round the new church building everyday for about six months in the early stages of the work. We believed that he was praying that there might be no further accident. He walked slowly, with eyes down-cast, looking at nobody and speaking to nobody. I was the only one he spoke to. The workmen had great respect for him and had great faith in his promise that there would be no more accidents.

It almost seems as if building was only possible at Mount Argus when Charles was in residence. The foundation stone of the church had been laid with great solemnity on 29 June 1866, just four days before Charles had been transferred to England, but it had remained alone and surrounded by weeds for eight years, waiting for him to return. Now that he was back at Mount Argus, supporting the work by his prayerful presence, the new church began to take shape.

On 28 April 1878 (at that time the feast of Saint Paul of the Cross), Dr McCabe, later Archbishop of Dublin, blessed the new Saint Paul's Church, Mount Argus. A Dublin newspaper carried this description of McCarthy's masterpiece:

It is a superb specimen of the majestic Romanesque style. The great western front flanked by campanile towers is pierced by three ample entrances, formed beneath an arch and moulded portico, above which are semicircular lunettes containing groups in high relief, representing scenes in the life of Saint Paul of the Cross; that on the left hand being Saint Paul while an infant, rescued by the Blessed Virgin from being drowned; in the centre the Blessed Virgin showing the habit and badge of the Congregation of the Passionists to Saint Paul; and at the right Pope Benedict XIV, approving of the Rule of the Congregation.

One of his contemporaries, a fellow-Passionist, tells us that 'God alone is cognisant of all that Father Charles did to make Mount Argus what it is. He alone knows the number and the value of his deeds which are so precious in Heaven's sight. The period from 1857 to 1893 (with the exception of a few years which he spent in England) were passed by him within its walls, and his name will ever be entwined with its history'. We can say of Charles, as was said of the man who built another Saint Paul's, 'If you seek his monument, look around you'.

VII

The Blessed Will of God

So far we have been looking at Charles more or less from the outside, observing his actions, seeing what he did at various times and in various places. We might ask ourselves what was going on behind the scenes we have witnessed. Every day Charles was coming into close contact with misery and sickness. What was all this pain doing to him?

It would have been easy for him, seeing so much human suffering and having to listen to so many people's problems, to become hardened, to begin to treat people in a routine or impersonal manner. Indeed at times he may have felt tempted to do so even as a means of survival. Instead, he is remembered by those who knew him as someone who was always open and accessible:

Father Charles was entirely at the disposal of the sick and poor and dying. He was greatly in demand by them. I myself came to him several times: he was always very kind and accessible.... All that interested him was that they were in trouble and needed his help which he gave most readily and effectively.

I myself recall his blessing me: he looked at me so kindly and laid his hand on my head and, child though I was, I felt that the man who blessed me was out of the ordinary, on a higher plane than others but still so accessible.

Father Charles' charity towards his neighbour was universally spoken of in Dublin in those days. He was much sought after by all kinds of people in sickness or trouble and he was at the disposal of all. Many a time on my police beat I was stopped by people inquiring when and where they could see Father Charles. I often marvelled at Father Charles' patience; he never showed any sign of impatience when he was so persistently and, as I sometimes felt, unreasonably followed by people. I often felt inclined to intervene and send them away, but he never showed any sign of being annoyed with them.

What was the secret behind this accessibility to which so many refer? What was the source of his patience, his openness to others? Rather than being hardened by his contact with suffering, Charles developed a deep sensitivity to the pain of others, a sensitivity which was rooted in his devotion to the Passion of Jesus. The Passionist Constitutions state, 'We seek the unity of our lives and apostolate in the Passion of Jesus. His Passion reveals the power of God which penetrates the world, destroying the power of evil and building up the Kingdom of God' (Chap. 5). For Charles the Passion was the link between his life and his apostolate; his ministry and his own personal life were the two complementary facets of his commitment to Christ crucified. Meeting Christ suffering in the poor, the sick and the dying, he was being drawn daily into a deeper participation in the mystery of Christ's Passion as it was lived out by others and as it was to be lived out by him.

His whole life of prayer was centred on Christ crucified. At Mass he often wept, especially at references to the Passion. Father Eugene Nevin, a member of the Mount Argus community who has left us his personal recollections of Charles, wrote:

The simplest discourse on the Passion moved Father Charles to tears. During the reading of the meditation which takes place every day in choir, it was touching and edifying to see him lean forward hand to ear straining to catch every word, eager that none of its golden treasure should be lost to him. Little needed he reminder of Calvary, for it was never absent from his thoughts. Nevertheless he invariably carried about him a small crucifix, sometimes placed on top of his little devotional manuals as seen in the photo, but more often locked in his left hand palm. From time to time he could be seen to open the hand, look affectionately at the crucifix and raise it tenderly to his lips. I saw it after his death showing signs of long and frequent use.

The Stations or Way of the Cross was one of his favourite devotions, though by no means an easy performance from the difficulty he experienced in kneeling and rising unsupported. But that only made it all the more dear to him. He generally practised the devotion in the seclusion of the religious choir or oratory, where he was free from any interruption or distraction, a luxury not likely to be allowed him in the public church.

Living far from his family, in a community where he could

never speak his own language, Charles had what was in some
ways a lonely life. Always having to express himself in English,
a foreign language which he never fully mastered, it was inevi-
table that he would at times experience a deep sense of isola-
tion. One of the community has remarked that 'although we all
loved and honoured him, he had no intimate friend. He gave
the impression of being lonely, though in reality of course that
could not be the case, for Christ was his constant companion'.
On 10 July 1878 his uncle wrote, inviting him to come home
on holiday and meet his brothers and sisters. Charles politely
turned down the invitation; such visits were not usual among
the Passionists at that time:

I have thought about the long journey by land and sea. After so
many years I hardly remember how to speak my own native tongue.
I hope to see you all again in heaven with Jesus and Mary, and all
the angels and saints.

Indeed his home was never far from his mind. In his letters to
his family we find that his brothers and sisters are constantly
in his prayers. Sometimes too his mind drifts back and he asks
for news about friends from his days in Munstergeleen, in-
dulging in a little nostalgia for the land of his birth. According
to Father Eugene, when Charles visited a house in Rathgar,
Dublin, in which there were many paintings,

there was one picture in particular, and it the least valuable of the
lot, which beyond all the others claimed his attention, and elicited
his emotions – a Dutch Winter Landscape. When he came upon
it for the first time he exclaimed, 'Ah, a Dutch painting!' and remained long looking at it and viewing it from every angle. On each

of his subsequent visits he acted in a precisely similar manner. The subject being a familiar one no doubt called up memories of his early associations, with pleasant recollections of the house where his childhood's days were spent.

Speaking of the Stations of the Cross, Father Eugene referred to the 'difficulty he [Charles] experienced in kneeling and rising unsupported'. This was the result of an accident which took place on the Tuesday of Holy Week, 12 April 1881. The cab in which Charles was travelling collided with another carriage and was overturned. He tried to jump clear but was caught under the cab and badly hurt. In his diary, Father Salvian writes that,

On last Tuesday Father Charles having jumped from a Jaunting Car, whilst in motion, he broke his leg at the ankle. Father Charles' absence from the Church during this busy time was felt very much, especially that we had to find out another to put in his place in singing the Passion on Good Friday, the Lamentations, etc. It is not expected that he will be able to get out from bed soon, which to him is of the greatest trial, on account of not being able to say Mass. On Maundy Thursday Holy Communion was brought to his room, with great solemnity. All the students accompanied the Blessed Sacrament with lighted candles.

Charles himself, in a letter to his brother, Father Peter, says, 'I must tell you that much to my regret I have broken my right foot. I was in great pain for three weeks and four days'. This fracture never healed properly and for the rest of his life Charles had difficulty in walking. Thomas McGrath, who was then a postulant at Mount Argus but later became a doctor, remembered the incident:

I was refectorian, and was to take a cup of coffee to Father Charles every morning during his illness. Fractures then were not as well treated as they are now, so that I think he must have suffered severely in the cold of the night. He must have suffered immensely from thirst. I found Father Charles in his usual ecstatic state. He used to try to deceive me by his smiles.

Father Salvian mentioned that because of the accident Charles was unable to take part in the singing of the Passion Gospel on Good Friday. This Holy Week he was being called upon to share in the Passion of Christ by his own suffering, uniting his pain to the pain of Christ. Father Eugene recalls for us the scene on other Good Fridays:

His part during the years I knew him was always that of Christus which suited his style of voice admirably. But it was still more in accord with his sentiments in that he had to sing the words of our Lord in the garden, in His trial, condemnation and death. His very appearance was striking as he entered the sanctuary accompanied by the two other priests appointed for the other parts.

... Entering wholeheartedly into the meaning and spirit of the words, Father Charles soon became lost to his surroundings, overwhelmed by grief in the sympathy he felt for the Divine Victim. There would be many long pauses, unrubrical it is true, but necessary to suppress the sob and wipe away those tears that dim the page.... There would be tears in more eyes than Father Charles' before he had finished, for no preacher could produce such effects as he did by his appearance and general bearing during his singing of the Passion. It was the important feature of the Mount Argus Holy Week services in those days.

In the Christian tradition there are two different ways of approaching human suffering; these are clearly expressed in the two Opening Prayers of the Mass for the Sick in the Roman Missal. The text of one prayer reads:

> All-powerful and ever-living God,
> the lasting health of all who believe in you
> hear us as we ask your loving help for the sick;
> restore their health, that they may again offer
> joyful thanks in your Church.

> *– Roman Missal*, p. 838

The other Opening Prayer, however, is not a prayer for healing but for the grace of acceptance. This prayer reminds us that Jesus accepted suffering to teach us the virtue of patience in human illness; it goes on to ask that all who suffer pain, illness or disease may realise that they are chosen by God and united with Christ for the salvation of our world.

Not all those who came to Charles for healing were cured physically; some he encouraged to bear their cross in union with Christ while others he advised to prepare for death. In ministering to the sick there is a great need for discernment, to know when we should pray for healing and when for acceptance. Charles realised that there were cases where the cross of suffering must be carried bravely. Writing to his sister Mary Christine he expressed the hope that she would

bear her illness with resignation, because this is God's will, and with devotion, since this will be to her advantage. She must not lose heart in her sufferings and should think of the Passion of our Lord Jesus Christ. Saint Paul says, 'The Lord chastises those whom he loves'. May my sister grow used to saying these words, 'Blessed be God! Thy will be done! I adore your holy will! My God, I thank you for this illness, for crosses, etc.'

On another occasion he wrote to his brother Peter,

I was sorry to hear that you have been ill. I hope you will recover soon. I was very pleased to hear that you have been totally resigned to God's will. Oh, holy will of God! May his will be always obeyed, honoured and blessed by men! Oh holy will, oh blessed will! Our happiness in this life and in the life to comes lies in carrying out God's will; as Jesus said, 'Here I am, Father; I come to do your will'.

This resignation in suffering was not just something to be preached to others; Charles had to learn its meaning in his own life. He had advised his sister not to lose heart in her sufferings but to think of the Passion of Christ, as he had learned to do. The exhausting nature of his ministry, the loneliness he often felt, the continual pain in his leg which was soon to be followed by other sicknesses: all these were for Charles opportunities of faith, invitations from Christ not to lose heart but to think of his Passion.

From about this time Charles' health began to deteriorate. On 23 January 1882 Salvian wrote in his diary, 'Poor Father Charles, not being well lately, has been dispensed from coming into the Choir for Matins and Prime'. Significantly, Charles had written to his nephew only two days earlier,

Let us ask the Infant Jesus to give us the virtue of patience and of complete submission to the will of God in all that we do and in all the suffering we have to bear, especially in our last illness and at the hour of our death. Let us ask him not only for the strength to resist temptation and persevere in his divine love, but also for the grace of being able to pray always, since through prayer we acquire divine love and perfection, perseverance and eternal happiness. May our divine saviour share the eternal glory of heaven with us. Amen.

On 10 August 1883 Charles' brother, Father Peter Joseph Houben, died; he was fifty-six years old, six years younger than Charles. In all, five of his brothers and sisters predeceased Charles, but perhaps he felt Peter's death more intensely than any of the others. Writing to his uncle, Charles said that he was deeply saddened by Peter's death but, he added, 'we must frequently call to mind that it is the holy will of God. From the beautiful letters he wrote to me I can say with certainty that he was a good and holy priest, and so we must hope that he has already tasted the joys of heaven'.

A fortnight later, Charles was still immersed in his grief; his mind was not really on what he was doing, much to the annoyance of Father Salvian who tells us in his diary that 'the monthly Procession was a regular confusion.... There was no organist. Father Charles intoned some extraordinary "Dutch Litany" which no one knew, and elicited general laughter, especially among the youngsters'. No doubt Salvian told Charles afterwards just what he thought of his 'Dutch Litany'. As always for Charles, his place of refuge was at the foot of the Cross, where his suffering and the sufferings of others could be seen in their true light, as he himself had written:

The Cross patiently borne for the love of God helps greatly for our eternal salvation.... Strive to think every day, for a few minutes, on the bitter sufferings of Jesus Christ.... May Jesus and Mary always reign in our hearts.

VIII

Pray Always

In the Passionist Constitutions we read that Saint Paul of the Cross 'wished his followers to pray without ceasing and desired our communities to become real schools of prayer, leading to a deep experience of God' (Chap. 37). This desire to fulfil the Gospel teaching that we should 'pray always and not lose heart' (Luke 18:1) was for Charles an important part of the legacy of the Founder of the Passionists, Father Columban Tyne recalled that 'his spirit of prayer was remarkable: his union with God and spirit of prayer were continual. He realised the command of our Lord that we should always pray. This was the most striking characteristic of his life'. Looking at the intense apostolic ministry which Charles exercised, we might be forgiven for wondering how he managed to pray at all; yet those who knew him affirm that he lived always in the presence of God. Patrick Hickey, who had been an altar boy at Mount Argus, gave evidence at the Apostolic Processes:

I recall Father Charles especially as a man of continuous prayer.

Wherever he was, passing along the corridors, etc., his lips continually moved: occasionally he would make an ejaculation aloud. We boys were greatly impressed by the sight of his continuous prayer. I never saw him but that he was praying. After his death, one of the religious here (I cannot recall his name) told me that Father Charles' knees were like huge knobs as a result of his long hours of kneeling in prayer.

The practice of the presence of God was a key element in Charles' life of prayer, as we see from his writings:

'I am with you till the consummation of the world', says our Lord to his Apostles. The Apostles in all the trials they had to endure could well say with truth that the Lord was with them. Being so fervent, so careful in the practice of the presence of God, they considered God constantly before their eyes. Let us endeavour in all our trials to have God before our eyes; the neglect of this practice has been the reason of so many faults.... Let us have God before our eyes day and night and we shall advance in perfection.

For Charles, attentiveness to God's presence was expressed in the long hours he spent each day in meditation. No matter how busy he was, he was always present for the Divine Office and for the two hours of meditation, the one in the morning and the other in the evening. From time to time the doctor would forbid him to attend the Night Office of Matins, which took place at two o'clock in the morning and was followed by meditation until three o'clock, but unless expressly dispensed he was sure to be at Matins.

Charles left no prayer journal or spiritual diary by means

of which we might examine his life of prayer to discover what was happening during those hours of meditation. However, in a letter written shortly after the twenty-fifth anniversary of his ordination, we are allowed for a moment to listen in as he reflects on the Incarnation and responds to God's gift of his Son:

During these holy days of Christmas, my thoughts were constantly on the priestly state; I thought, too, of the Incarnation of our Lord Jesus Christ, of the ardent wishes and desires with which the saints of the old law awaited the coming of the Messiah, since God in his mercy had promised to send a redeemer to man, fallen and condemned to hell. These saints of the old testament prayed without ceasing to hasten his coming. Had they the happiness of seeing him, what would they not have done to please our Saviour? How fervent they would have been in showing their love for him, how zealous in showing gratitude for all the graces and blessings he had come to bring them. The birth of our Lord Jesus Christ in the stable at Bethlehem is a mystery, it is a miracle so great, abounding so much in humility and love, that it will be wondered at by the angels and saints in heaven for all eternity. What can I, a mere man, give the Divine Redeemer in return for such great and innumerable blessings – so great that they cannot be explained – which, for so many years, I have received from his mercy? When I consider this, I feel urged to thank God with greater fervour, to please him more, and to do and suffer everything willingly for his love and for his greater glory.

Contemplating the mystery of the Incarnation, a 'miracle so great, abounding in humility and love', Charles felt moved to respond generously to God and 'to do and suffer everything willingly for his love and for his greater glory'. In his later years he had frequent opportunities of suffering for the glory of God as his health continued to deteriorate, partly because he was getting older but also as a result of the constant demands being made on him both by the people to whom he ministered and by the rigours imposed by the Passionist Rule, with its emphasis on penance and mortification, fasting and vigils.

During the 1880s Charles was under the additional strain of living as a member of a community which was in crisis. The constant building work at Mount Argus, the construction of the monastery and later that of the church, had left its mark not just on the grounds but on the men who lived there. For twenty years much of the energy of the community had been poured into the building and into trying to pay off the debt which, by the standards of the time, was enormous. In a report to the Superior General written on 5 December 1878, just seven months after the opening of the church, the Provincial, Father Alphonsus O'Neill, said that the debt on Mount Argus was £24,331 and he informed the General that the community were barely able to support themselves and pay the interest on the loan; the debt, he says, 'is breaking the hearts of Superiors, occupying and I might say wasting lives and energies that should be employed in higher and holier work'. Fundraising to meet the debt was a constant activity of the community during those years, often involving absence from prayer and other community exercises. According to Father Salvian,

the fervour of our religious began to fall at the Bazaar and Grand Distribution of Premiums of 1869, when almost all our Fathers and Brothers were engaged in travelling 'selling tickets' for the Grand Bazaar. All observance [i.e. community prayer] was almost given up, in this Retreat especially. From that date to this we have not risen as yet to the level in which we were previous to that.

A succession of Rectors had tried to lower the debt and raise the fervour but it seemed very difficult to succeed in both. At one stage Father Alphonsus, in an attempt to take some of the weight off the shoulders of the Rector and Vicar (i.e. the Vice-Rector, who also acted as Bursar), had separated the debt on the buildings from the ordinary income and expenditure of the community and had made Father Sebastian Keens, who had formerly been Vicar, responsible for this new account. This decision was later to cause its own problems, as we shall see.

In 1879 the Superior General, Blessed Bernard Mary Silvestrelli, had visited the Province. At Mount Argus he had met Charles and, according to Father Eugene Nevin, the General was 'deeply impressed by his spirit of prayer and the degree of his union with God'. However, his overall impression of the Province was less favourable. In a circular letter written at the end of the visitation he says, 'Whilst on the one hand we do not accept as true, and we do not believe all the reports that have been spread abroad regarding the Religious of this Province, on the other hand we cannot deny the evident fact that many things said have had foundations'. Three years later, in August 1882, Father Bernard Mary was still concerned about what he saw as the absence of religious life among the Passionists of Britain and Ireland. At a meeting of the General Curia in Rome he spoke of the lack of leadership on the part of the superiors of the Province who, he said, were the first to neglect the Rule; he suggested that the only way to raise standards in the Province would be to bring the students, immediately after the Novitiate, to Rome where they could be formed in a more prayerful atmosphere, far away from the 'laxity' of Ireland and England.

Within this general context Charles' insistence on fidelity to prayer, a frequent theme of his letters, takes on a fuller significance. The single-mindedness and determination which had helped him during his schooldays were needed once more if he was to keep his head when all around were losing theirs. Writing to his uncle in August 1883 he says,

Pray at all times, desiring that God's will be accomplished completely in your regard. From the Imitation of Christ, by Thomas à Kempis, we learn to ask our good, merciful God for these graces: the graces of prayer and perseverance; prayer and a happy death. As Saint Augustine says, be sure that the divine mercy will never abandon you provided that you persevere in prayer.

The situation at Mount Argus had been difficult for some time, but what actually brought matters to a head began at the Provincial Chapter on 21 July 1884 when Father Jerome Smith was elected Rector of Saint Paul's Retreat. Father Jerome was forty years of age at the time; ordained fourteen years earlier, he had been working as a missionary in Bulgaria since shortly after his ordination. Described by those who knew him as a 'true man of God', who had 'a noble, unselfish nature which enshrined many a trait of which the best might boast', he was unfortunately ill-suited to the role of superior and had virtually no administrative ability. His obituary says that his 'chief characteristic was zeal for souls'; this is borne out by the fact that he spent a great deal of time preaching missions, an unfortunate consequence of which was that the community was often left to stand on its own feet, which it was scarcely capable of doing. According to Salvian, Father Jerome began well: 'At the Friday Chapter Father Rector spoke about the observance which is very much neglected.... If it was not for the Students, we might nail up the Choir door. Many a time the poor students are alone in the Choir'. The new Rector also employed a man to answer the doorbell because, Salvian tells us,

Complaints from our friends, and strangers, were reported constantly of being left in the Parlour for hours, or for having been ringing the bell for a long, long time before the door was opened. ... Over and over again the Fathers have complained to the Superiors or to the Provincial, who spoke to the Porter of the time being, but they might have spoken to the pillars outside the Hall Door. It is true that the bell is ringing almost continually and it requires the patience of a saint to attend at every call. It is also true that the poor Porter has to ring or sound the gong 3, 4, 5, 6 times before the Religious who are called go down which indeed is very provoking. During the time that the Porter is waiting for the Religious who is called, the bell is ringing perhaps three or four times, and of course the people who are ringing get annoyed and go away. Hundreds of people come every day for the blessing by Father Charles....

Two smart men would scarcely be enough to attend properly our Hall Door.

The hundreds of people coming every day for the blessing of Father Charles were tiring not just the porter but of course Charles himself. Just two weeks after Father Jerome's arrival, we read in Salvian's diary:

Poor Father Charles is not well at all and should not be allowed for some time to get up at Matins, and even to say the office at all, being extremely weak, and his poor head, as he says, 'is going round'. When he says Mass he trembles and shakes, as if he was affected by the ague. He should not be put down for public Masses, not being really able, part for scruples, and part for weakness. To give communions to the people is out of the question entirely, he would shake and tremble, as to let the ciborium fall from his hands. When he has to say public Masses, I always attend him in surplice and stole, and give the communions to the people myself. If I was not there, even if he had not to give communions, he would take more than an hour to say Mass. It is true, he is not put down for public Masses except in extreme necessity, but even then he must be attended by some priest to prevent an accident. The saintly man never complains when he is appointed to say public Masses or to act as Deacon at High Mass every Sunday. He, generally speaking, says Mass on Sundays and weekdays at the altar of Saint Mary Magdalene, and some priest or other is near him, but if he should be entirely alone, with a boy server, he would spend on the altar an hour or so, as it has happened on several occasions. It is wonderful how poor Father Charles can stand the going up and down fifty-nine steps, hundreds of times every day, to bless the people, who come by crowds for his blessing. Many are the cures and real miracles which take place, but we never take notice of them, and much less Father Charles take any notice. Every Sunday after the High Mass, and again in the afternoon after Vespers, he goes into the Church and blesses with the Relic of Saint Paul of the Cross, at the average of seventy or eighty people, besides those which he blesses in the Parlour. The fame of Father Charles' holiness is spread throughout Ireland, England and Scotland, and even in America. Several persons came to Dublin from America, and England for his blessing and to be cured from some disease or other. Enough at present about Father Charles. For the future I intend to take notices about him, as they will be interesting for the Chronicles.

A fortnight later Charles, who was obviously much run down, became very sick; as a consequence he was not able to say Mass or do any work for about three weeks.

Father Charles was ill the whole day, being tormented with diarrhea, sickness of stomach, and lightness in his head. He could not eat any nourishing food, but only an egg and a few spoonfuls of brandy. There is no mistake, the dear poor Father is getting weaker and weaker every day, and unless he is sent away from home, even for a fortnight, or a month, we shall lose him. Like a Saint, he never complains, and never tells any one what he suffers, only that we find out by the way he walks, and the appearance of his countenance. After the evening service, as I did not see him, I went to look for him, and found that he was in the Closets, sick as could be. I brought him to his room, gave him a little brandy, and put him into bed. Father Vicar ordered him to obey me, and so he did, without delay.

Towards the end of the month Salvian notes that 'Father Charles is getting better, but he will not be able to say Mass as yet. No Matins last night, nor the night before. I said it alone at the usual hour [2 AM].... When Brother Isidore was here, he sounded the rattle and rang the bells, for the sake of keeping up the observance, at least externally, for in reality only Father Charles, Isidore himself, Brother Mark and I attended the Choir'. In spite of his poor health, Charles continued to struggle on, trying to be faithful to his ministry without in any way neglecting his prayer. Listing the works of the community in his summary for the year 1884, Salvian includes 'the blessing of hundreds of people by poor Father Charles although the saintly man is very feeble, and has sores in his legs, and ache in his head and teeth'.

In this condition, his going up and down the fifty-nine steps from the parlour to his top-floor room and back again many times a day and his constant fidelity to prayer, especially the night Office of Matins, were a concrete living out of his desire 'to please God more and more, and to do and suffer everything willingly for his love and for his greater glory'. Charles epitomises that quiet heroism which we could describe, borrowing words from another writer and another context, as a 'lonely fidelity to an abandoned ideal'. We can picture him during these years of trial as he was remembered by Mary Cooke at the Apostolic Processes:

He was very spent-looking, thin and bent with infirmity, or rather as a result of his habitual attitude of prayer. I remember Father Charles' infirm appearance, which suggested that he really should have been in his sick bed: instead, he laboured incessantly, praying and blessing the people.

IX

The Struggle is Continual

Among the most important sources of information about Charles are the writings of Father Salvian. Apart from his personal diary, Salvian also kept the *Platea*, the official chronicles of the monastery, for almost twenty years. A man who held strong views on most subjects, Salvian was quick to notice the failings of others and left many sharp comments on human nature not just in his diary but also in the *Platea*. He took special notice of Charles, as he has already told us, because of his reputation for holiness; another man he kept his eye on, but for a different reason, was Father Sebastian Keens.

Father Sebastian, or the 'Great Man' as Salvian liked to call him, was probably, after Charles, the best-known Passionist in nineteenth-century Ireland. He was for many years the Director of the Confraternity of the Passion, which he had introduced into Ireland, and was the author-editor of a number of prayer manuals some of which were best sellers. In great demand as a preacher, he gave retreats and missions all over Ireland and was considered an excellent preacher by everyone; that is, everyone except Father Salvian who, even back in 1874, had written in his diary:

The [May] Procession in the afternoon went on still better than the Sunday before. Father Sebastian preached one of his 'anything and everything' sermons, and made himself a great fool in his theatrical delivery. The contortions, the tone of voice, the eternal repetition of the same things over and over again *usque ad nauseam* tired everyone, except perhaps some old woman who understood nothing of the sermon, except the screams and the stamping of the feet of the preacher. What a pity that people will not listen to the good advice of others!

When Father Jerome Smith became Rector in July 1884 Father Sebastian, who was then fifty-two years old, was at the height of his popularity. On close terms with many of the prominent figures in Dublin society, he had organised some very spectacular events in aid of Mount Argus, with a little help from his more influential friends. Although a man of great ability, he was never made Rector of Mount Argus, which no doubt surprised him greatly but was a comfort to many in the community. However, he had managed to work himself into a position in the community where he could act more or less independently of the Rector even within the monastery; taking advantage of Father Jerome's lack of experience, he now began to act as if he were in fact the superior. In the house chronicles Salvian has left this account of the Feast of Saint Sebastian, 20 January 1885:

The Mill-house at Munstergeleen, birthplace of Saint Charles

John Andrew Houben, First Infantry Regiment

St Wilfrid's Retreat, Cotton Hall

Father Osmund Maguire CP

Mount Argus – the original farmhouse with the old church

The men who built Mount Argus

The Church which was never built: McCarthy's original design for Saint Paul's Church, Mount Argus

Handbill distributed by Brother Michael Behan when he and Father Charles went questing for the new church

Father Ignatius Spencer CP

Mount Argus community in 1864. Back row (l. to r.): Saint Charles, Father Osmund Maguire,
Father Ignatius Spencer and the Superior General, Father Peter Paul Cayro

Saint Charles at Mount
Argus; photograph taken
in the 1860s

Father Jerome Smith CP,
Rector of Mount Argus
1884–1886

Brother Michael Behan CP,
companion of Saint Charles

Father Salvian Nardocci CP,
Chronicler of Mount Argus

Back in Dublin: Charles in the 1870s

Father Sebastian Keens CP,
the 'Great Man'

Father Dominic O'Neill CP, Rector of Mount Argus
at the time of the death of Saint Charles

The 59 steps Saint Charles went
up and down to bless the sick

Saint Charles' room, now used as a chapel

Photograph of Saint Charles taken shortly before his death

MOUNT ARGUS. DUBLIN 769. W. L.

Saint Paul's Retreat: the open window on the second floor
(sixth from the left) is that of the room where Saint Charles died

Tomb of Saint Charles: Bust by Marjorie Fitzgibbon, ARHA

Pope Benedict XVI announcing the date of the canonisation of Saint Charles of Mount Argus

Canonisation of Saint Charles, 3 June 2007

Early in the morning the students presented an address to the Rev. Father Sebastian, who was seated in a rich armchair, under a beautiful throne [i.e. canopy], which had been put up by the same students in their recreation room. Tablecloths were laid in the Refectory; Father Sebastian took the first seat at table, and acted as Superior the whole day. This is never done, even for Father General.

In the evening, after supper, the community was invited upstairs to the Throne Room where there was a grand display of good things in the shape of Cakes, Tarts, Biscuits, Native and Foreign Fruits, Wines of different sorts, but especially the 'Native'. Then speeches, songs and recitations until a late hour. It was a splendid 'Fete' and the students especially enjoyed it very much.

The writer does not exactly, nor necessarily agree to all this sort of thing being done on the Feast of a private individual, unless the individual is one of the Superiors.

Whether from motives of kindness or weakness, Father Jerome was inclined to leave Sebastian unchallenged. While it was true that he was working to raise money to pay off the debts of the monastery, it was equally true that he had effectively cut himself off from the day-to-day life of the house, being always absent from community prayer and spiritual conferences, and from community meetings unless the business under discussion affected him personally. The acts of largesse in which he indulged during Father Jerome's rectorship tended to antagonise some members of the community, who resented his playing the role of superior and wondered where the money for the feasts was coming from. His strongest allies were the students who always treated him with deference and respect, though sometimes not from the purest of motives, as we learn from a diary kept by one of them, Adrian Cole:

25 November 1885. Today is the thirtieth anniversary of Father Sebastian's ordination. An address was delivered by Confrater Ambrose containing of course sentiments that would be 'truly noble' in Father Sebastian's estimation, such as when he was styled in it a 'pillar of the Church' and 'worthy to wear the mitre', etc. This oration produced its desired effect and we spent a very pleasant evening in the professed recreation, everything being provided by Father Sebastian, and of course well seasoned with compliments.

The students were delighted to have some entertainment and were quite willing to pay the price. However, not everyone in the community was as pleased as they were with Father Sebastian's generosity. Salvian gives this version of the proceedings, and his comments:

The students presented him [Sebastian] with an address full of praises and flattery, which the good Father swallowed with the greatest delight. In the evening after the service he regaled the whole community with sweets, cakes, apples, grapes &c, and whiskey and wine to swallow them. Speeches, replies, songs in abundance *usque ad nauseam*. Well, I do not know what to say about this sort of things. If they were done to honour our Superiors on the Silver or Golden Jubilee, well and right, but when they are repeated three times a year, viz. at the anniversary of the Clothing or Profession – at the Feast of the Patron Saint – and at the ordination, and done with such publicity, and I may say dissipation, I cannot reconcile myself, nor could I approve such things.

Father Jerome's inability to take a firm hand in situations

began to show itself in other ways. The general atmosphere of neglect which had been building up in the community over the years now came to the surface. There was a careless attitude towards the church, with priests failing to appear for Masses and other public services. The house itself was not even clean; the kitchen was dirty and untidy and the corridors were in need of sweeping. This external carelessness was symptomatic of a deep feeling of hopelessness and futility within the community, faced as it was with the depressing reality of a financial situation which was completely out of control; this was being further aggravated by the crisis of leadership in the house. The Provincial, Father Vincent Grogan, at the Visitation in September 1885, had made a vain attempt to shore up the external structures of the community: 'He spoke very strongly but most kindly about the abuses. Most solemnly he prohibited the use of spirits before dinner; recommended the punctual attention to the Choir night and day; attention to the confessional; and abstaining from smoking in the rooms'. In noting these admonitions of Father Vincent in his diary, Salvian was unable to resist a footnote on Sebastian: 'Strange to say, my friend who has not put his foot into the Choir since the Visitation of twelve months ago, except on two or three occasions for Prime and Tierce only, was not present even on this occasion'.

The strong but kind words of the Provincial did nothing to stop the downward slide which was now well under way. There was no lack of good will on the part of members of the community, as Salvian says, but good will alone was not sufficient. In his summary at the end of the year 1885 he admits that

the observance of many points of our holy Rules and Regulations are disgracefully neglected. The Choir, day or night, is attended only by the students and one or two of the priests. There is no recreation in common; only few attend it. There are some who very seldom are seen in the Choir for Sext and None, Vespers or Compline. If you happen to pass on the low level corridor during that time, you will see them by twos or threes chatting away, as unconcerned about the Choir as if it was their business to stay away.

The 'one or two of the priests' attending the community prayer were Salvian himself and Charles, when he was able. Charles was still subject to bouts of ill-health and according to Salvian 'had become very weak, and his mind a little affected', as a consequence of which he was sent, on 23 July 1885, to Holy Cross Retreat, Ardoyne, Belfast for a few weeks' rest. Brother Michael was sent with him, to take care of him. However, Charles had very little rest in Belfast; news of his arrival leaked out and within a short time the monastery was besieged by people asking for him. According to P. J. Tiernan, who was an altarboy at Holy Cross at the time, 'During the period Father Charles was at Ardoyne enormous crowds of people from all parts of the North of Ireland came daily, some afflicted physically or otherwise and others in perfect health, to be blessed by him'. With this state of affairs Charles was probably busier during this 'holiday' than he would have been had he stayed in Dublin. When he returned to Dublin on 11 August there was, according to Salvian, very little improvement to be seen: 'The saintly man seems a little better, but in my opinion not much. I fear that if the poor Father is allowed again to bless the people who come here from every part of Ireland and England for his blessing, he will again get as bad as before'.

While he was genuinely concerned about Charles' health, Salvian was also glad to see him back; he had been given the job of blessing the people while Charles was away and had found them very demanding, as a result of which he had tried to put some order on the proceedings:

During his absence I was appointed to bless the people, and I was not left a moment to myself. There was a constant up and down the whole blessed day, from morning till evening, when I was at home. I dare say that every day more than fifty or sixty people come for the blessing and on Sunday there must be more than one hundred; however, I made a regulation on this point and fixed hours when I would go down, in the Old Chapel, and bless all those who were there.... In particular cases I went down in the Parlour and blessed them there. If Father Charles is put under obedience to do the same, I think it will answer very nicely, without distress. The Porter should not call him except at these hours.

Later that year, during the first weeks of November, Salvian was again called upon to replace Charles, who was unable to move because of rheumatism: 'I had a great many of them for the blessing or, as the poor people say, for rubbing with the relic of Saint Paul'.

Salvian mentioned that he had been blessing the people in

the old church, which had been left standing when the present church was opened in 1878. Two months before Charles' visit to Belfast the students had set up a grotto of our Lady of Lourdes inside the old church; here it was that Charles was now to bless the people, although occasionally he would also give the blessing at the altar of Saint Mary Magdalene. It is interesting to note that the times for the daily blessing with the relic of Saint Paul of the Cross (10.30 AM and 4.00 PM) were fixed not by Charles but by Salvian.

The new year 1886 brought no remarkable improvement either in the bodily health of Charles or in the spiritual health of the community. In the month of March, two days before the feast of Saint Patrick, Father Sebastian managed to find another way of upsetting the community. The student Adrian Cole tells us that 'Father Sebastian got permission from the Father Rector to have an old panegyric of his upon Saint Patrick read in the refectory. He preached it twenty-two years ago in a church, Melior Saint, London. I think most of the priests are offended by this almost unprecedented act'. A few days later there was a community celebration for the feast-day of Father Gabriel, the Director of Students, at which, according to Adrian, 'Father Sebastian got up and made a long speech on Father Gabriel's virtues, alluding to the time when Father Gabriel was Rector of this house, and he was his Vicar. When he had finished, Father Pius [Devine] started to his feet, and gave Father Sebastian some very sharp words about his conduct as Vicar, respecting Father Gabriel. Father Sebastian left a few minutes afterwards'. Sebastian's combination of naivety and pomposity had turned most of the priests of the community against him; three days later he succeeded in doing the same with the students:

Father Sebastian came to our recreation this evening with a great secret which could not be divulged unless all the students were present. When most of us were there, he told us that [he] desired very much that we should form a kind of committee to have for its object the publication of his sermon on Saint Patrick that was read in the refectory and also the other one that he preached on last Saint Patrick's day, as they would tend very much to increase faith and patriotism, and for this purpose we should speak to the Father Rector *only*. He then produced a manuscript on which most of his last sermon was written out, but as I have not reached the practise of virtue in the heroic degree, and consequently could not remain listening to such stuff for an hour or so, I very thoughtfully remarked that one or two students were absent.... I went out to find them, taking remarkably good care not to return.

In the months which followed, Father Jerome's authority in the community continued to diminish until finally he decided that the only course of action open to him was to resign his office. He wrote to the Provincial offering his resignation and it was readily accepted. The Provincial then wrote to Mount Argus, informing the community and appointing the Vicar, Father Anselm, as interim superior, with Father Salvian as provicar, until a new rector would be elected by the Provincial Curia. When the letter arrived, Father Jerome was away, giving a mission. In fact, wrote Adrian Cole, he 'has been giving missions uninterruptedly for the last four or five weeks, so that his powers were virtually suspended, and I suppose his resignation was expected as a matter of course'. In the same letter the Provincial, Father Vincent Grogan, announced that he would arrive in Dublin the following Monday, 16 August, to conduct the Visitation of the monastery. According to Adrian Cole, the students believed 'that this Visitation will be very severe'.

On 13 August, three days after the letter from the Provincial had been read publicly in the Choir, Charles wrote to his brothers and sisters, 'Thank you very much for your lovely letter.... I am very well and everything is fine'. In the context of the situation at Mount Argus – the Rector's resignation, the coming of the Provincial, the anxiety in the community, and the general background of turmoil and confusion – his words 'everything is fine' seem laughable at first sight; but as the letter goes on, we see how his preoccupation is not with surface problems but with deeper realities:

Let us abide and remain in the sweet hearts of Jesus and Mary, and let us ask the Blessed Virgin every day to obtain for us, through her powerful intercession, a real spirit of prayer and the gift of perseverance in prayer to the end of our days; may she obtain for us a happy death. Amen.

In praying for a real spirit of prayer and the gift of perseverance Charles reduces the problems around him to the most fundamental level; indeed by his own persevering fidelity he was during these difficult times a silent, yet strong, example to all the others of what it means to be a disciple of Christ.

On Monday 16 August Father Vincent opened the Visitation. He told the community that he had been summoned to appear before the Archbishop, Dr Walsh, on account of complaints which had been made against the Passionists. In Salvian's diary we read:

Reports are gone to the Archbishop against us, which seem to be rather serious, and we fear will bring great disgrace upon this community. May God protect us. In this diary, I have occasionally remarked some internal irregularities, but I never would have dreamed that more serious ones would have been brought before the Archbishop. What these accusations are, I do not know, but from the way that the poor Father Provincial spoke, I fear they are serious enough. The crisis seems to have come, when the poor Provincial will have to act with strong hand, so contrary to his kind, mild and fatherly dispositions.

During the Visitation the Provincial addressed the community, speaking on the values of Passionist religious life and emphasising the importance of prayer, solitude, mortification and recollection. When he came to examine the financial state of the house, he found things to be in a very bad way; he wrote the following comments in the Account Book:

On examining this Book, we find the financial statement handed in at the Visitation to be a deplorable revelation. The Vicar who endeavoured to keep this book, could not in conscience sign it, as the late Rector was not careful in giving him an account of money received and money paid out. The House has gone in debt to an alarming degree since last Visitation, and there must have been a reckless extravagance. However under a new regime there is every hope that a better report will appear next year. There is no knowing the real state of affairs, as according to the present statement, the deficiency not accounted for is £259 three shillings and eleven pence. The Rector is to blame and no one else.

Father Vincent concluded the Visitation on Friday 20 August, after having given what Salvian describes as 'a magnificent address, telling us of the innumerable abuses he had found existing in this Retreat, at the same time earnestly beseeching us to put an end to these sort of things and live as good Passionists'. Father Vincent had also asked Salvian to refrain from writing criticisms of individual members of the community into the *Platea* as this would 'not remedy the evil but exasperate the feelings of the guilty'. While agreeing to do as he had been asked, Salvian explained his point of view in his diary: 'When there was anything that was not right, I had no human respect; I spoke strongly in the said Chronicles, as anyone who may read them will find out. When we shall have a superior who will "do" first and "teach" after, it will be all right' (31 August 1886).

All were now wondering who would be the new Rector. There was a great deal of talk and different names were put forward. The general feeling was that the most suitable person would be Father Bernard O'Loughlin, who was at that time the Master of Novices. Father Bernard, who was sixty-three years old, was a remarkable man; Salvian described him as 'one of our best religious in every way'. A man of great experience, he had at different times been Vicar, Rector, Provincial Consultor and Provincial. According to Salvian, he had also been Commissioner General for the Franco-Belgian Province, had been the first superior in Paris, where he had built the Church and Retreat, and had been the first superior of the first Passionist foundation in Spain. It was said in Mount Argus that he 'would be the only one who could be appointed with advantage to this community. Two or three of the old Fathers went farther in their opinion, and said that Father Bernard would be the only one who could save this Retreat from utter destruction' (*Platea*).

After a month of waiting, on 14 September a telegram arrived from the Provincial. 'About six o'clock p.m. the news came that Father Bernard was elected Rector of this house; this was expected by a good many, but it was doubtful whether he would accept it' (Adrian Cole, Diary). Three days later Father Bernard arrived at Mount Argus. The following day, the Provincial

installed the new Rector into his Office with the usual ceremonial. Then the whole community paid him their obedience, and all showed their gladness for the happy event. After this the new Rector addressed a few words of encouragement in the practice of virtue, but especially on the faithful observance of our Holy Rules, and promised us that if we do so, we shall be happy here, and hereafter.   – *Platea*

When the news of Father Bernard's election had come, Salvian had noted in his diary: 'The general opinion in this Retreat is that Father Bernard is the very man who will be able to revive the spirit of the Passionists in this house and to remedy its financial affairs'. The hopes of Salvian and other members of the community did not prove to be vain. Father Bernard began by going round the garden 'pulling up old withered shrubs', but his desire to clean up Mount Argus went beyond the garden. By encouragement and by example he began to rebuild the community's sense of purpose and to heal the divisions which had arisen within the house. Under his leadership the spiritual life of the community began to flourish once more, as Salvian tells us: 'Our present Rector is very prudent and is the first in all the observances; he has already brought us back to the primitive fervour in many points, and by degrees he will complete the full reformation.'

The 1880s were difficult years for the community of Saint Paul's Retreat. The members of the community reacted to the situation in different ways; some used it to their own advantage, while for others it was a source of annoyance and feelings of bitterness. There were those who opted out of the life of the community, and those who found their consolation in complaining, or in more harmful pursuits. One man stands out during this period, conspicuous by his faithful witness to the importance of prayer and apostolic service. For Charles these must have been years of great suffering, as he lived through this experience of fragmentation and collapse in the community. However they were for him also years of growth: growth in self-knowledge and growth in faith. Some months after

Father Bernard's arrival, when things had begun to improve, Charles wrote to his family, 'I see now just how necessary prayer is in order to practise all the virtues in their perfection'. He was well aware of the harm which had been caused by the absence of prayer in the community and, consequently, more convinced than ever of the need to fulfil the Lord's command to 'pray always and not lose heart', as he writes in the same letter:

How greatly has God loved men! He did not spare his only Son but abandoned him to death, even death on the cross. Jesus Christ urges us to pray; but how? Ask, seek and knock. It is for this reason that the Lord has said: 'Watch and pray, lest you fall into temptation.' Let us listen to the words of Thomas à Kempis: 'My son, in this life you will never be completely free or without fear, but as long as you live, make sure you are spiritually armed, because you are living in the midst of enemies who are attacking from every side.'

'The struggle is continual', says Saint Bonaventure; it is for this reason that we must pray during our whole life.

X

At the Hour of My Death

During the last years of his life Charles was constantly aware of the nearness of death. Living as we do in an age when it is considered almost rude to speak about death, his frequent references to death seem strange to us, accustomed as we are to avoid such a topic. In the letter to his brothers and sisters quoted above he says,

I am an old man now and am afraid of death. I pray daily that through the powerful intercession of his Mother, God in his mercy will grant me a happy death. Sixty members of the Passionist order have died in Ireland and England since I came over here from Belgium.

The death of his brother Father Peter Joseph had a profound effect on Charles; in almost every letter written to his family after Peter Joseph's death, Charles speaks about his own death and asks for prayers that he might have a happy death. In a letter to his sister Anne Mary he writes,

I'm afraid that I will die soon; in your kindness pray for me, that the good God may grant me a happy death and a favourable judgment. I pray for you all continually that he may grant you the same grace. It is helpful for us to say often the Act of Contrition and also the words of Saint Francis de Sales: 'My Saviour Jesus Christ, by the merits of your Sacred Passion and your most holy Death, give me the grace of perfect contrition for my sins, so that I may never offend or displease you again.'

Our separation will not last much longer. Let us hope that we will meet again in heaven. Amen.

Fear of death is a fundamental human experience; it is something with which each of us must struggle. According to the Second Vatican Council, 'It is in the face of death that the riddle of human existence becomes most acute. Not only is man tormented by pain and by the advancing deterioration of his body, but even more so by a dread of perpetual extinction' (*Gaudium et Spes*, Chap. 18). Nevertheless, the Council document goes on to say, 'to every thoughtful man a solidly established faith provides the answer to his anxiety about what the future holds for him'.

It can be said of Charles that the pattern of his life was shaped by his awareness of death. Death for him was not an abstraction – 'All men are mortal' – but an existential reality – 'I too must die'. This understanding of the transitory nature of our earthly life he tried to bring to others, as we see from a story he told in one of his sermons:

A certain nobleman went to the Pope to make his confession to him. When he had finished, the Pope gave him a penance, but he said that the penance was too hard. Then the Pope said to him, 'Say

once a day, "I shall die one day"'. The nobleman accepted the penance. He performed that little penance, and afterwards he lived a
most holy life.

Fr Eugene Nevin recalls that Charles was often heard to pray,
'O Lord, let your Passion be so realised and verified in me that
I may never die in sin.' Father Eugene tells us that Charles
would also say, 'So many communions; so many Masses; so
many Confessions, yet how sinful I am. Will I ever be saved?
Will I ever get to heaven?'. Coming from the lips of one who
was living such a heroic Christian life these words seem shock-
ing at first sight, but this was no false humility throwing scorn
on itself. Charles was deeply aware that he was a sinner who
must plead for mercy. According to Father Eugene,

There was then not far from the monastery a brick field, whose furnaces looked fierce and threatening in the darkness of the night. Of
a Winter's evening he used to take a position at one of the windows
commanding a view of them, and remain long in meditative mood.
If accosted, as I know he was, now and again, he would point in the
direction of the furnaces and say 'See!' And then after a pause 'O!
the sufferings of the lost, and I deserve all for my sins. O! God be
merciful to me a sinner.' After another pause, and borrowing the
words of Saint Augustine for the expression of thoughts similar to
his, he would exclaim *Hic seca, hic ure, sed parce in æternum* (Wound
and burn me here, but spare me in eternity) beating his breast
the while.

Charles' deep awareness of the reality of sin was not the result
of a morbid preoccupation with self; in the light of his deep
spirit of prayer and his compassion for the suffering, he could
not be thought of as self-centred. Nor did his sense of sin

come from any distorted notion of God, as we can see from one of his letters:

All God's blessings are infinite, but the effects of his grace are more abundant than anything. For that reason Saint Paul calls God rich in mercy. He is called the Father of mercy and grace, but never the Father of justice and severity.

The true sense of sin which comes from God is rooted not in our own feelings of guilt but in the experience of the truth of God's merciful love. It was because he knew the reality of God's love for him, the love which is shown on the Cross, that Charles was able to say from the depths of his heart, 'O God, be merciful to me a sinner.'

In his sermons Charles frequently spoke of sin which he described as 'a monster which cannot be seen'. He would encourage the people who came for his blessing to love and serve God most fervently, because 'we must lead a holy life if we wish to die a holy death'. 'How dreadful must it be', he would say, 'to have concealed mortal sins in confession. How terrible must it be for those damned souls at the first appearance of the Judge.' For Charles sin was a 'black ingratitude' by which God is 'despised, mocked and derided':

We should all be dead to sin and live only to serve and love God. God has placed us in this world not to live according to our own will, nor to follow our bad inclinations; our body and soul and all our faculties must be employed to please God. The early Christians could indeed flatter themselves that by keeping themselves in such a rigorous way of living, in praying, fasting, in performing other austerities, they avoided sin with so great a care. Alas, that happy time is no more. Now sin is committed everywhere; in all places, in all states of life, they commit sin like they swallow water. What hatred you should have against sin! You should consider that sin is rebelling against God and a black ingratitude to the divine Majesty. Now a creature most noble, created to the image of God, created to serve and to love, revolts against his Creator. But, my dear brethren, consider well that sin ought to be feared more than anything in this world because the sinner who commits a mortal sin becomes the enemy of God. He does all in his power to destroy his God and causes a black ingratitude, after having received so many benefits from God.... especially in this country in comparison with other countries. God who is your Father, your Master, your Benefactor is despised, mocked and derided; he is made to suffer, having favoured you so kindly. If you would ever see a person taking his crucifix in his hands and trampling it under his feet, you should say, 'What a wicked person this is.' Now, a person who commits a mortal sin does far worse.

After demonstrating how terrible sin is, Charles would urge his hearers to turn to Jesus, whose death on the Cross gives us the power to overcome our sinful inclinations:

The means to become perfect is to mortify our predominant passion. As a Captain in the time of battle, in order to gain the victory, endeavours to arrange the soldiers at that point where he sees the greatest dangers are to be overcome, so we should do the same. As long as we strive to overcome our little passions, we shall not be easily overcome by the strong ones.

What is the means to be used to overcome our passions? It is to meditate on the Passion of our Lord. A person who is proud, for instance: if he sees that Jesus Christ is derided, mocked, sent from one place to the other and keeping silence, he sees a great motive of humility in Our Lord. Another is impatient: he may look to the Crucifix and he will find a model of patience.

Among Charles' writings is a paragraph entitled 'The Comparison of a Soul in the State of Grace and a Soul who is in the State of Mortal Sin'. In this text he begins by describing the happiness of the person who is in the state of grace. This person, he says, can address the Redeemer as 'spouse, dove, sister or brother'. In contrast, the person who is in a state of mortal sin has turned away from God:

At the hour of death that soul having committed so many mortal sins, to whom shall she turn her eyes? To the eternal Father, being so long despised? To the Son, being so many times crucified? Or to the Angels, being always ready to lift up their sword to punish that soul? Or to the Saints who participate in the glory of the happiness of heaven? To whom then must she turn her eyes? Ah, to the Mother of God, Mary, the only Refuge of sinners. We have recourse to thee, O Mary!

For Charles, Mary was the 'Refuge of Sinners', the one to whom he could turn for help in time of need. He saw her as the model for the Christian, an example to be imitated by those who wish to live as disciples of Jesus: 'We should love and serve the Blessed Virgin, and imitate her virtues. She ought to be our book, our model, our mother.'

Father Eugene Nevin tells us that 'his devotion to Mary combined the simplicity of a child with all the strength and constancy of which his firm character was capable.' Among the few books he kept in his room were the *Treatise on True Devotion to the Blessed Virgin* and the *Secret of Mary* by Saint

Louis Marie de Montfort; he used to recommend these to others. According to his confessor, Father Norbert McGettigan, 'He would speak of the great Mother of God as his "own dear Mother", and the sweet name of Mary was always on his lips. When he spoke of her Immaculate Conception or her sufferings at the foot of the Cross of her divine Son, his face would light up with unusual brilliancy.' Above all, Mary was for him the one in whom we trust 'now and at the hour of our death', as we see from one of his prayers:

O my great Angel Guardian and my Patron Saint, and all you holy angels and saints, unite your prayers to mine, and together let us beseech our glorious and heavenly Queen to obtain for me all the most efficacious graces that I may never commit any wilful sin; and that she may receive me as her child, guide my steps through this sinful world, assist me at the hour of my death, obtain for me a very happy one with a favourable judgment, and conduct my soul to the Throne of God, there to enjoy the glory of the most adorable Trinity. Amen.

Father Eugene witnessed an unusual incident towards the end of Charles' life which gave him an appreciation of the depth of Charles' love for the Mother of God. It took place in the refectory at Mount Argus. Usually during meals there was a reading from the life of a saint or some other spiritual book, except on fast days when the evening collation was taken in silence:

Everything was going on as usual, the customary silence being observed, but through the silence came the softly whispered ejaculations of Father Charles.

Suddenly he started up from his seat with wonderful agility calling aloud the name 'Mary, Mary'. Throwing down his serviette, placing his left hand over his heart, with right extended on high, he became transfixed and motionless as a statue, his upturned gaze fixed on a point in the lofty ceiling. I looked, all looked, at the same point expecting to see something. We, of course, saw nothing, but a thrill of awe went through everyone for we felt that something extraordinary had happened. For some moments, moments seem hours in some of the events of life, he remained in that ecstatic attitude, fit subject for the artist's brush, until the Superior brought him back to himself by calling out loudly 'Father Charles, Father Charles! You are disturbing the Community!' Then he resumed his former position as if nothing out of the common had occurred.

Charles had first arrived in Ireland on the feast of Mary, Mother of Holy Hope, a feast which is proper to the Passionist Congregation. The picture of the Mother of Holy Hope shows Mary and, in her arms, the child Jesus who holds a cross in his left hand; it reminds us of the saying of Saint Paul of the Cross, 'The whole life of Jesus was a cross. The whole life of one who serves God, then, should be to remain on the cross with Jesus'. The mission of Saint Charles of Mount Argus, which began on this feast of Mary, was to bring healing and hope to the crucified ones of this world: the poor, the lonely, the sick, the dying. To them he would frequently say, 'Have faith; pray to Mary'. His aim was to bring the people to whom he ministered closer to Jesus, and to do so through Mary.

Faced with the awareness of his own sinfulness and, in his last years, the nearness of death, all his trust was placed in Jesus our Hope and in Mary his Mother. Like Saint Paul of the

Cross he could say, 'All my hope is in the Passion of Jesus and the Sorrows of Mary'. Among his papers, after his death, was found a prayer he had written which expresses his trust in the mercy of Jesus and the protection of Mary; this prayer, which he said every day, he calls a 'Prayer to the Blessed Virgin to obtain a Good Death':

Mary, sweet refuge of miserable sinners, when my soul is on the point of leaving this world, oh my most sweet Mother, by that sorrow which thou didst endure when assisting at the death of thy Son on the Cross, assist me with thy mercy. Drive the infernal enemy far from me, and do thou come and take my soul to thyself and present it to the eternal Judge. My Queen, abandon me not. You, after Jesus, hast to be my comfort in that terrible moment. Entreat thy beloved Son in his Goodness, to grant me the grace to die clinging to thy feet, and to breathe forth my soul in his wounds, saying, "Jesus and Mary I give you my heart and my soul". Amen.

XI

The Renowned and
Saintly Father Charles

When Father Bernard O'Loughlin became Rector of Saint
Paul's Retreat, Charles was in his sixty-fifth year; he had
only six more years to live. These last six years of his life were
marked by two progressive developments, one external and
the other internal. Externally, he was becoming more and
more of a celebrity in the eyes of the people, while interiorly
he was growing less and less concerned about day-to-day matters, a natural part of growing old, and increasingly absorbed
in God. However, this deepening of his spirit of recollection
was not without its dangers:

Poor Father Charles had an accident which might indeed have
been rather serious, but his Guardian Angel protected him. He
fell into a hole, in the closets, about six or seven feet deep. The
plumbers, who are at present repairing the pipes for water, had
taken up a trap door and left it open. Poor Father Charles, who is
always wrought up in God, did not see the danger, and down he

went, straight into the hole. He complains only of a little pain, and of the fright he had. – Diary of Father Salvian, 16 February 1887

The May Processions through the monastery grounds, always considered an important event in the Dublin calendar, became during these years opportunities for the people to express not only their love for Mary but also their veneration for the man they called 'Father Charles of Mount Argus'. Father Salvian gives this account of the Procession which took place on 1 May 1887:

Grand Procession at four o'clock in honour of our Blessed Lady. The whole service consisted in Solemn Vespers, Sermon by Father Rector Bernard in the Church, Procession, and Benediction with the Blessed Sacrament. Father Charles officiated at Vespers, and at the Procession, carrying the Relic of our Blessed Lady. It was a wonderful and edifying spectacle to see the people by thousands kneeling on the ground and saying to each other, 'Here is Father Charles – that is Father Charles – may God protect the holy Saint', and so on. I heard and saw it, being near Father Charles, more to protect him from being crushed by the crowd, who would have thrown themselves at his feet to kiss his habit, than to keep the Procession in order.

from time to time there would be references to Charles and his ministry in the newspapers. *The Irish Catholic*, describing the Crib which had been set up at Mount Argus for Christmas 1888, said, 'It is erected in the little wooden chapel in which the renowned and saintly Father Charles has performed innumerable miraculous cures upon persons afflicted with all manner of diseases'. An English Catholic newspaper also told its readers about the old church at Mount Argus and the happenings there:

This shell of a building, which exteriorly looks like an old schoolhouse, is the scene of constant pilgrimages. Hither come or are led from time to time, the blind, the lame, and the halt to supplicate their cure at the hands of Father Charles Houben ... to whom popular belief has ascribed the possession of the Apostolic gift of healing; and, I am credibly informed, instances are not infrequent which furnish a practical commentary on the text of Saint James: 'The prayer of faith shall heal the sick'.

Father Eugene Nevin recalls that 'from all parts of the English-speaking world letters came to him by every post requesting his prayers and blessing in illness or distress of whatsoever kind.... The people's faith and confidence in the efficacy of his prayers and blessing was so great that they believed almost all things possible to him'. Yet, according to Father Eugene, 'he himself was the greatest miracle, living all those years so wholly dedicated to his vocation'.

The Rector had, at Father Salvian's insistence, appointed certain times in the day when those who wished to be blessed by Charles should present themselves in the old church. Father Eugene tells us that the people would gather there every day waiting for Charles to arrive:

A little ahead of the appointed times a leaning and pensive figure would be seen to emerge by slow degrees from beneath the pillared portal of the Monastery door, seemingly oblivious to all such contingencies as arrangements of time and place. Sometimes little

as precise the Father leading his child along the
precipice ... this Father leaves the child alone
the child will fall in   and die. God the best.
...

Prayer to the Blessed Virgin
to obtain a good death

Mary sweet refuge of miserable sinners,
to whom my soul is ... the point of
leaving this world oh my most sweet
Mother by that sorrow which thou didst
endure when assisting at the death of
thy Son on the cross, assist me with
thy mercy. Drive the infernal
enemy far from me and do thou
come and take my soul to thyself
and present it to the eternal ...

Prayer to the Blessed Virgin to obtain a good death. Saint Charles' own handwritten copy.

Judge. My Queen abandon me
not. Then, after Jesus hath it
be my comfort in that terrible
moment. Entreat thy beloved
Son, in his goodness, to grant me
the grace to die clinging to thy
feet, and to breath forth
my soul in his wounds saying
Jesus and Mary. I give you
my ~~soul~~ Heart and my soul.
                              Amen

Blessed are the poor in spirit for theirs is the
Kingdom of Heaven).

The Pharisees confessed only once and not
with their own hands be ~~of~~ Religious who
would commit a mortal sin confess. A
soul with his own hands a religious who falls
often in mortal sin will never be converted
he relapses now considerate, he falls
from precipice to precipice he falls
completely into ruin the malice which
he has to offend our God is almost infinitely
greater than that of a secular person
who commits a mortal sin
medicine too of exaltation cos of oppression
& pass nourished them than I have exalted them
and they have despised me

groups would be waiting, sometimes none, for the people naturally collected where they knew they were sure to meet him. But
in a few moments, as if by magic, ones and twos and threes would
come out, apparently from nowhere, grouping themselves around
him, the men uncovering, the women in prayerful attitude. Grown
soon to fair proportions a go-as-you-please procession moved in
the direction of the old church, so slowly that the distance of less
than a hundred paces ordinarily took about half an hour. This was
because he made of it a miniature Via Dolorosa or road to Calvary
with many stopping places where he got the people to meditate on
scenes in the Passion, and repeat after him prayers in honour of the
Sufferings of Christ and the Sorrows of his Blessed Mother.

When he arrived in the little church, Charles would first kneel
almost prostrate for about five minutes before turning to address the people. Thomas McGrath recalled how effective his
words were:

I heard Father Charles preach, I recall his intense earnestness: he
seemed to want to reach out and grasp every soul in the congregation.... He was a very remarkable preacher, possessed of a powerful
voice; he gesticulated very much, was inclined to preach too long.
... Often he seemed to be overcome by his own emotions and earnestness. The congregation was likewise affected by his words: they
listened to him most attentively, and occasionally a sigh or moan
would be heard in sympathy with the preacher's own emotion.

In his preaching he would urge his listeners to be converted
to Christ, to turn away from sin and be faithful to the Gospel.
'Remember', he would say, quoting Saint Bernard, 'that the
Lord seeks not only flowers but fruits, that is not only good
desires and resolutions but also holy works.'

When he had finished preaching, he would prepare the people to receive the blessing with the relic of Saint Paul of the Cross by inviting them to renounce the Devil, afterwards sprinkling them with holy water. According to one witness, 'he would accompany his words by stamping on the ground as if he were actually trampling on the Evil One'. Charles understood that there can at times be a link between bodily sickness and the powers of evil, as we see from this prayer he offered for a woman who was paralysed:

O Blessed and Immaculate Queen of Purity, thou who from the beginning hast received from God the power and might to crush the head of Satan, humbly we beseech thee to send thy Holy Angels that under thy power they may pursue and encounter on every side the evil spirits, resist their bold attacks and drive them hence into the abyss of everlasting woe. Amen.

When those present had renounced the Devil, Charles would begin to pray aloud, partly from a book and partly extempore. This prayer would go on for some time, after which he would give the blessing with the relic of Saint Paul of the Cross, praying that God, through the intercession of Saint Paul, would free those present 'from every evil of mind, soul and body, in the name of the Father and of the Son and of the Holy Spirit'. According to Father Francis Kelly, 'when he was imparting the blessing, he would look up to heaven and a radiant smile would suffuse that face which was at all other times so serious'. After this, he would pass through the crowd, blessing those who were sick and praying over them. Mary Agnes Styles, who was cured at Mount Argus in 1892, remembered the intensity of his prayer:

Father Charles came and knelt on the ground beside me for a long time: then he rose and blessed me with something he had in his hand. Then he knelt down again and prayed most intensely, the beads of perspiration standing out on his forehead.

Although the Rector had fixed the times for receiving the blessing with the relic, Charles' compassion was not constrained by the timetable: 'after giving the relic to the people in the church, if some people came late he would go out again for the relic patiently'. Others still would come to the monastery outside of the regular times; Father Columban Tyne recalled his cheerfulness and patience on those occasions:

At the time I knew him, when he was seventy years old, he was infirm as a result of his years and failing health; yet he would come down from his room at the top of the house most cheerfully and readily every time he was called for – probably many times a day. This must have been most trying and exhausting. He was patient with the ignorant, compassionate to the sick and scrupulous; the poor he especially loved.

Even in these last years of his life, when so many people were coming to see him at Mount Argus, he was still willing, in spite of his poor health, to visit sick people in their homes when called upon. Stephen Dempsey tells how when his father was seriously ill, his mother went to Mount Argus for help:

My mother, who was in despair, came to Father Charles who accompanied her back to the house: on the way Father Charles repeatedly said, 'A stroke! God help us.' I don't know how he knew what was wrong with my father. I remember my father during his illness: he was lying in bed, scarcely able to move or speak. When Father Charles came, he prayed over him for nearly a quarter of an hour. Father Charles before leaving told my father to get up. He did so and dressed himself without any help: everybody was astonished when they saw my father up and walking about as if he had never been ill.

In her moment of anguish Stephen Dempsey's mother had turned to Charles, as did many others at all times of the day and night. When told that his cousin was dying, Owen Mc-Donald, an officer in the Dublin Metropolitan Constabulary, went in the middle of the night to ask for Charles' prayers; he arrived at Mount Argus when the community were chanting Matins.

When my cousin James McDonald was very seriously ill, in fact according to the authorities of the Richmond Hospital dying of Typhoid fever, in 1891, I came here [to Mount Argus] to get Father Charles' prayers. It was about 2.30 AM and the Brother who opened the door told me to write down what I wanted. I did so and he took it to Father Charles. He returned after some minutes and told me, 'Father Charles says your cousin will be all right.' When I got back to the Hospital the nurse (who had previously been the means of sending me to Mount Argus, since as she said, 'your cousin is dying and there is nothing you can do now except to go to Father Charles') said to me: 'I know the exact time you were with Father Charles, because your cousin took a turn for the better at that moment.' My cousin improved hourly and is still alive. I always attributed my cousin's recovery to Father Charles' prayer. The hour in which he surmounted the crisis of the fever exactly coincided with the hour at which I sent up my written petition to Father Charles.

During these last years Charles was always in the public eye. Shortly before his death, he happened to be in Westland Row railway station waiting for a train; some people in the crowd recognised him and within a few moments he was surrounded by a large crowd kneeling on the platform, asking for his blessing. Yet in spite of being the centre of attention wherever he went, Charles never lost that simplicity of heart which put those who met him immediately at their ease. Owen McDonald, who as a policeman worked in the area around Mount Argus stated:

Father Charles was the most humble man I ever knew. He seemed to have no opinion of himself, free from all ostentation. He certainly did not seem to be in any way puffed-up by the fact that so many people came to see him.

XII

Poor Old Charlie

Poor Father Charles is getting more and more obstinate in his ways by keeping the people too long waiting for him, and when he goes he keeps them for hours on their knees, shouting like an energumen, reading prayers of his own which the people do not understand. The saintly man has not the common sense to see how much he inconveniences the poor people who come by hundreds every day. Unless something is done for poor Father Charles, he will lose his brain entirely. He never comes to recreation with the community, never takes a little walk in the garden or any other place. He keeps his eyes always closed, and never sees what is going on before him, being constantly wrought up in prayer – and if you speak to him, he seems not to understand what you say.

Writing in his diary in July 1890, Father Salvian was very concerned about what Charles was doing. Nor is this an isolated passage in the diary; during the last years of Charles' life, Salvian expresses from time to time his unhappiness with Charles' ways of doing things. A little earlier he had expressed his annoyance at what he saw as Charles' refusal to listen to him:

I am constantly advising him, but I may spare my breath; his ob-

stinancy is worse than that of a mule. The poor man is really religiously mad, and should not be allowed to say Mass or to bless the
people in the way he does. No doubt he is not responsible for what
he does, but the Superiors should look to it. Many people come
for his blessing every day, and on Sundays by hundreds, being considered a living saint, and indeed such he would be if he would be
guided by others.

Since, as he saw it, the superiors were failing in their duty by
not keeping Charles under control, Salvian had made it his
business to act as his advisor and help him to arrange his life.
He had already succeeded in giving him a timetable by per-
suading the Rector to have fixed times for the blessing; now he
felt that something should be done about how he conducted
himself on these occasions, but in this he was having less success:

He never takes the advice of anyone; his impression about sanctity
seems to be in reading some prayers which he has found in devotional books or pamphlets, and you cannot convince him that some
of these prayers are not approved by the Church and there are no
indulgences attached to them. Every day he spends hours morning and evening in reading these prayers before blessing the people,
who come by hundreds, and he shouts at them like an energumen,
evidently not knowing what he is doing. The poor saintly man is
doing everything with the best of intentions, but he will not listen
to the advice of anyone and continues to do his own will.

Salvian could never understand why Charles would not take
his advice. Only a few months younger than Charles, he had

been his superior at Cotton Hall and at Sutton; they had been members of the same community for more than twenty years. Who, then, would have known Charles better than he did? Who, in his own opinion, could be more suited to act as Charles' advisor? For reasons such as these, but also for reasons of temperament, Salvian took it upon himself to keep Charles on the right path. He began to play a dominant role in Charles' life, not only giving him unsolicited advice but also correcting him publicly for any unbecoming conduct as he saw it. Father Benedict Donegan, who as a young priest was stationed at Mount Argus in 1891, remembered an incident which occured at a *Gaudeamus* or recreation day: 'Father Charles was singing and Father Salvian ordered him under obedience to stop, a thing he had no authority to do. Father Charles obeyed instantly and showed no sign of resentment'.

So good was Father Salvian at his work that it came to be believed in the community that he had been officially appointed to act in this way by no less a person than the Superior General, Blessed Bernard Mary Silvestrelli. Father Eugene, in his recollections, reflects the common opinion which was held by the community when he says that the General 'commissioned Father Salvian to closely watch Father Charles, take note of anything extraordinary in his life, and as occasion served, to put his virtue to the proof'. In fact Salvian makes no mention of his having received such a commission in any of his writings. Usually in the diary he makes a particular point of noting any responsibilities given to him by his superiors; we can scarcely believe that he would have been given this task by the Superior General and yet have failed to refer to it in his diary.

Father Eugene recalls that there were times when Father Salvian pushed Charles almost to the limits of his endurance:

He would correct him, scold him and humiliate him before the whole community, thus adding immensely, I am sure, to his merit, for of course Father Charles knew nothing of Father General's secret instructions. He never showed the least sign of resentment; nor did he seek to explain himself but remained silent and penitent, looking as if he had been guilty of some great crime. If he did speak at all he confined himself to the three words 'poor old Charlie'.

Usually Charles was able to see the funny side of things when Salvian tried to put him right. Father Eugene remembered one occasion when Salvian 'rounded him in right royal fashion before us students about some imaginary fault'. At the height of his outburst Salvian turned round and stormed away. With a smile on his face, Charles 'pointed after his well-meaning tormentor, then tapped his own forehead with his forefinger', indicating to the students that they should not take the incident too seriously. 'Small wonder indeed', adds Father Eugene, 'if he had begun to think Father Salvian's mental balance was getting a bit disturbed'.

Undoubtedly Father Salvian acted in this way believing that he was doing what was best for Charles. Although a man of strong opinions, there was never any hint of malice or cruelty in his character. On the contrary, he was noted for being kind and considerate. However when things were not going his way, he was inclined to explode and at such times he was capable of trying the patience of a saint, as Father Bernard Mangan tells us: 'I remember once that Father Charles cut him rather short on an occasion when Father Salvian corrected him, but you could not say he was angry or in a temper: it was like a gesture of impatience'. According to Father Bernard, Charles was 'quite urbane and could take a joke', but obviously this time the joke had gone too far. Usually, however, he was able to take Father Salvian's 'help' in his stride, using the scolding he received as an opportunity to imitate Jesus who remained silent before his accusers; from Charles' own writings we can see the pattern he tried to follow on these occasions:

Only those who wish to be trampled upon, ridiculed, humbled, who bear their cross daily after Jesus, who walk in his footsteps after his example, who imitate him will be saved.

The picture Father Salvian paints of Charles during the last years of his life would bring joy to the heart of any devil's advocate: religiously mad, shouting like an energumen – a demoniac, causing great inconvenience to the people (who, in spite of this, continued to come in their hundreds!), more obstinate than a mule. To what extent were Father Salvian's statements accurate? Was Charles a man of God or a religious maniac? Was he a saint or just a pious fraud? At the Ordinary Processes a number of his fellow-Passionists were questioned about this; here are some of the replies:

There could be no question of want of mental balance: he was quiet and calm. He was undoubtedly emphatic in his public prayers, but this I feel sure was due to his great fervour.

— Father Francis Kelly

I always regarded him as a sensible, sane man. There was something of extravagance in his actions, but you would say they fitted in to his character and were not laughable in him as they might be in others: they were the natural expression of his genuine religious fervour. He was out of the ordinary but only as a saint could be.

— Father Benedict Donegan

I would certainly affirm that there was no such thing as ostentation in the man. He was so openly genuine that it would be impossible to suspect him of any deception. I believe that his only foolishness was the foolishness of sanctity. He was self-sacrificing in his attention to the poor. I never saw anything that was really laughable in him; rather he was always edifying.

— Father Cyprian Meagher

No member of the community regarded him as being a fraud. There was no suspicion of ostentation in Father Charles' sanctity. All the time he was rapt in God. There was no suspicion of his being unbalanced. His actions might have been regarded as abnormal in another, but in him they seemed to be the natural expression of his great sanctity.

— Father Malachy Gavin

These testimonies are all from Passionists who were members of the Mount Argus community during the last years of Charles' life. These men, coming into close contact with him every day, were perhaps in a better position to say what kind of man he really was than were the people, who generally speaking only saw him in church. What was it like to live in the same house as 'Father Charles of Mount Argus'? How did the members of the community see him?

He was quite affable and liked by all. I never knew anything against his obedience: I would be surprised to hear anything such.
– Father Bernard Mangan

It could certainly be said of him that his every conscious thought or act was directed to God. He was certainly holier than the holiest person I have ever known.
– Father Benedict Donegan

He was always affable to all who came to see him, especially the poor. The very sight of the man did good. He sought no recognition or precedence. I never saw him give any sign of annoyance. He was always kind.
– Father Francis Kelly

If he had any predominant fault, I would say it would be a little temper or impatience. This was my impression deduced, for example, from the way in which he pulled away from those people who sometimes tried to pluck his cloak. This seemed to me to be an indication of his strong mind. He was not a man to be trifled with. He was not morose. He used to take part in the recreations of the community. One would feel quite at home in his company.
– Father Malachy Gavin

Father Malachy Gavin, who at that time was a student, says that he 'held the common view of Father Charles' sanctity'. However, that did not stop him, and other students, making fun of Charles from time to time. On one occasion, when one of the priests in the community was sick, some of the 'lighter spirits' sent Charles to his room to bless him: 'The Father was surprised and told Father Charles to go away. This humiliation Father Charles bore humbly' (Father Cyprian Meagher). Father Malachy tells us how, one morning, he happened to be alone in the coffee-room with Charles: 'I began twitting Father Charles on the common talk concerning his miraculous powers. I asked him if he worked miracles'. Father Malachy goes on to say that Charles replied by turning the conversation: staring intently at the coffee-pot, he simply said, 'He who made you made me'; 'from this', says Father Malachy, 'I understood that he did not wish to be questioned in the matter'.

In his testimony at the Ordinary Processes, Father Francis Kelly gives the following general impression of Charles:

My recollection of Father Charles is as of one never out of the Presence of God. He was a man of simple faith. If his exterior appearances represented his soul, then he was entirely on fire with the love of God. He possessed the prudence of pure simplicity; he was a man entirely without guile. I think in general he was a very mortified man; the poor creature never seemed to seek for anything. He was most uncomplaining, even when unreasonable demands were made on his services, as they constantly were. I am inclined to say that fortitude was pre-eminently one of his virtues, even heroically. He bore opposition and trials for the love of God. There may have been criticism of his ways. Father Salvian was severe on him. I heard that he was instructed to try Father Charles in this way. Father Charles bore this with his usual patience. He was remarkably obedient, even in hard things. He observed poverty fully. He

was a man of great delicacy in everything pertaining to chastity. He
was the essence of humility and kindliness. I do think that these
virtues were practised by him in a heroic degree, especially his mortification and zeal. His fervour was unbroken. All my knowledge is
purely personal.

Father Francis' description gives us a picture of Charles as
he remembers him during the years 1890-1892, when Father
Francis was stationed at Mount Argus, just after his ordination. During these years, as was remarked earlier, Charles was
becoming more and more absorbed in God so that to those
around him his life seemed almost to be a continuous prayer.
After the night Office of Matins, when the rest of the community went back to their rooms to sleep, he would often remain in the Choir, continuing his prayer until the morning
Office at six o'clock. When the Office and morning meditation were over he would celebrate Mass usually, towards the
end of his life, in the Choir. There is in Mount Argus a stone
stairway leading from the Choir sacristy to the organ gallery
in the Church; here, kneeling on the steps, where there was
less chance of his being disturbed, he would make his thanks-
giving after Mass, normally remaining there for about an hour.
According to Father Francis, he never lost an opportunity of
visiting the Blessed Sacrament. It used to be said that he always went to the Church when not detained by another duty;
in the afternoon 'during the "siesta" allowed to the Fathers he
would go to the Church to pray' (Thomas McGrath). Father
Eugene recalled that at night and in the winter evenings his
spare time was spent chiefly in the Choir.

Father Eugene also remembered what he called Charles' 'devout demeanour' as he entered the Choir:

With left hand far into one corner of his biretta, which he held closely up to his face, he would dip rather deeply the fingers of his right in the holy water stoup and fairly drench his forehead over. Then with measured step while in the act of crossing himself he proceeded to the centre, his leaning figure bending profoundly low. By reason of the accident, to which allusion has been made elsewhere, he was unable to genuflect without support. He therefore walked straight to the altar, laid his hand on its lowest step, went down on one knee, at the same time generally saying aloud, 'Jesus! Jesus!' Rising by aid of his right hand support, and making a graceful bow towards the Tabernacle he passed on to his accustomed place in the stalls.

In the years before his death, Charles' state of being 'constantly wrought up in God', as Father Salvian put it, was most noticeable during his celebration of Mass, which usually lasted an hour.

His devotion at Mass was remarkable, so much so that, at times, after the Consecration, I think, he seemed to get lost in contemplation and the server would have to pluck the vestments to recall him.

— Father Bernard Mangan

So often did Charles become lost in prayer while celebrating Mass that the altar servers were not surprised when it happened and knew exactly what to do:

I thought he was in an ecstasy often and had to pull his vestment. His

Mass one morning took an hour and ten minutes. I did not think that he was continuing the Mass while in an ecstasy: he seemed at certain times to discontinue the Mass. These interruptions would last sometimes five minutes, sometimes ten, sometimes fifteen or twenty minutes or more. These interruptions occurred in all his Masses. This I heard from the other boys. His Mass was never less than three-quarters of an hour. It was one interruption in each Mass, generally before the Consecration. Father Charles remained perfectly still. He did not seem to me as if he was praying: he appeared to remain quite still. There was no sign of his being raised from the ground. He did not speak or seem to read or make any exclamation during these silences. I was about fifteen when I used to serve his Mass. I often plucked his vestment and often without effect. He never resented this plucking of the vestment. The plucking seemed to rouse him to his duty. His not responding, as sometimes occurred, to these intimations seemed to me as a boy to be due to an ecstasy; it was due to his not having noticed, or to the fact that he was not conscious of his surroundings. The pluck we were accustomed to give was not very gentle by any means.

– Thomas McGrath

Because of the length of time he took for Mass, Charles normally said Mass privately in the Choir or sometimes at the altar of Saint Mary Magdalene. On one occasion shortly before his death, most of the priests of the community were away on missions and Charles had to celebrate one of the public Masses on Sunday; however, not all present counted it a privilege to be there:

I only saw him say Mass once. He was so devout that he had to

126

have two priests to keep him from being lost in ecstasy. It took him more than an hour to finish the Mass. In fact, after Mass, I heard some people say they would not come to Mass here any more because he was so long. But, such people would never be satisfied, no matter how quick the priest was.

– James Joseph Whelan

'When more than usually fervent by reason of the feast or from some other cause', recalls Father Eugene, 'the pauses became more frequent and progress in consequence more slow'. When this would happen in the Choir, the students serving the Mass would begin to get anxious because if the Mass lasted too long they would be late for classes and also would possibly have to miss breakfast. If the plucking of his vestments failed to have the desired effect on Charles, as a last resort one of the students would go for Father Salvian. Father Eugene describes what would follow:

Word is brought to Father Salvian, who on entering takes a small stole from his breast pocket, throws it on and stands beside Father Charles on the praedella. The effect is always electrical. Not a word for the present is spoken; but Father Charles well knows the meaning of the manoeuvre; and he needs not to be told to hurry up, for hurry he does in no unmistakeable fashion under the reproachful eyes of his mentor. Soon however a stronger influence governs him, and under its sway the figure standing close to him becomes shadowy and gradually fades away, when he is again alone with God giving way to demonstrations as before. But Father Salvian is never slow to remind him of his presence by a gentle tap on the shoulder and a mild if not a trifle profane command, 'Go on, Charlie, go on.'

Charles' state during his celebration of Mass was an expression of his basic attitude of attentiveness to the presence of God, which he had sought to cultivate from the beginnings of his religious life and, indeed, even before that. Throughout his life his aim was to keep God before his eyes in all his activities. What we hear described towards the end of his life as ecstasies were moments when the sense of God's presence became so overpowering for him that the awareness of anything else was for the moment pushed aside. Yet these moments, privileged though they were, must be seen within the context of Charles' whole life of prayer and apostolic service. In his desire to live a life like that of the apostles Charles kept Jesus Crucified always before his eyes; even in the refectory he would place his little crucifix on the table before him. In recognising the presence of Jesus living within his own heart and in the hearts of those to whom he ministered he succeeded in finding God in all things, echoing in his own life the teaching of the first great Apostle of Ireland, Saint Patrick:

> *Christ be with me, Christ within me,*
> *Christ behind me, Christ before me,*
> *Christ beside me, Christ to win me,*
> *Christ to comfort and restore me,*
> *Christ beneath me, Christ above me,*
> *Christ in quiet, Christ in danger,*
> *Christ in hearts of all that love me,*
> *Christ in mouth of friend and stranger.*

XIII

A Most Exemplary
and Beloved Priest

As the year 1892 drew to a close, it became obvious that Charles' life too was coming to an end. Although he was just seventy years old, Father Eugene Nevin tells us that 'his poor emaciated body was so worn-out that he looked fully ten years beyond his actual age'. According to Father Eugene,

For some time previous to his last illness it was plain to all his brethren that he was far from well. His slow movements and the only partial success of his efforts to conceal a halt were clear indications of it. Then he began to be late at the acts of observance owing to his inability to draw himself along in time, and absent altogether from some.

On 8 December, the feast of the Immaculate Conception, he celebrated Mass for the last time. The next day, a Friday, he was not able to say Mass but in the afternoon he came to the Choir for the weekly Chapter, though he was scarcely able to walk; genuflecting to go to his place, 'he had to lean his two hands on the Altar Step to enable himself to rise again. I can recall him very clearly as he was that afternoon because we all noticed how ill he looked, and subsequently spoke of it among ourselves' (Father Eugene Nevin). That evening when the community assembled in the refectory for the evening collation, Charles' place was empty. Father Salvian tells us what happened then:

Father Charles not having come into the Refectory for supper, the Infirmarian went to his room, to ask Father Charles what was the matter with him. At first he would not answer, but said that he would be all right in a few minutes. The Infirmarian asked him the cause of his difficulty in walking; he answered that he had pain in his leg. The Brother wished to see the affected leg and, behold, found it very much inflamed with a large sore. Of course he ordered Father Charles to stay in his room. I was there and we both requested him to lay down in bed, but he promised that he would do so bye and bye. The supper was brought into his room, but I heard that poor Father Charles took very little.

Father Eugene says that this sore was in fact due to Charles' injury years earlier when he was thrown from a carriage at Harold's Cross Green, and that the wound he had received on that occasion, which had never healed properly, had now become 'inflamed and angry-looking, and spreading its harmful influence through the whole system soon menaced his very life'.

Father Norbert McGettigan, Charles' confessor, had recently taken Father Salvian's place as Chronicler; it was he who noted Charles' illness in the *Platea*:

For some weeks, indeed for some months past, it was remarked that his strength was rapidly failing, as he seemed to walk with much difficulty, and was frequently seen to lean for support when walking from place to place in the Retreat. But in as much as he made no complaint, nor admitted that he was suffering any pain when asked, no particular notice was taken further than that it was the natural consequence of age and its consequent infirmities. However on the evening of the ninth the Brother Infirmarian, Brother Placid, suspecting that he was suffering great pain, insisted on knowing the cause, and found that his right leg from the knee to the ankle was fearfully swelled and angry-looking. The good father remained in bed next morning, and the doctor having arrived at an early hour, declared that he was suffering from erysipelas, which must have been neglected for a length of time, and hence would be very difficult to prevent its spread through the whole system. All was done that could be done, but the doctor, a good Catholic, had such slender hope of his recovery, that he recommended he should receive the Last Sacraments. He received the news of his critical state with calmness and resignation, and began at once to prepare himself. In the afternoon of the same day he received the Last Sacraments with great devotion, the whole community being present. The next day, Sunday, he was somewhat better, and during the week, but little hope could be entertained of his recovery.

In fact, according to Salvian, when Brother Placid had gone to Charles' room that morning he had found him lying on the floor; Charles had fallen out of bed and, being too weak to move, had lain there all night. That evening, when Salvian visited him he noticed that 'the dear soul was a great deal better, although not able to speak. Father Norbert, his confessor, is constantly at his bedside. All the Fathers and Students, besides the Infirmarian and other Lay Brothers, visit him very often. The Doctor came again at 10 PM'. Dr Murphy stayed with Charles until midnight, and through the night two of the community remained in his room with him.

The next day, Sunday, the Rector, Father Dominic O'Neill, asked Salvian to give the blessing with the relic to the people who had come looking for Charles:

During the day I blessed the people in the place of Father Charles, being appointed by Father Rector to do so for some days. To say the truth, I don't like to take such a duty upon myself. There is not much sanctity in me to work miracles.

– Diary of Father Salvian, 11 December 1892

On 14 December Salvian wrote, 'Dear Father Charles is going on suffering, truly like a Saint, and it is the greatest edification to the whole community'. The next day he noted, 'Father Charles continues to be very ill, and suffering very much, but no complaint ever escapes his lips'. Father Bernard Mangan later recalled his patience and resignation in suffering: 'During his last illness I was especially struck by his resignation to God's will. 'I cooperate with God's will' was his way of putting it. He suffered very severely but very patiently.... His habit of prayer and invocation was uninterrupted by his sufferings'. Father Columban Tyne remembered some of his prayers during his illness: '"My Jesus, I embrace this affliction for love of you. I desire to suffer in order to please you". Such and other prayers he constantly uttered and would get the students to join him'. Charles' attitude during his illness impressed not just the community but also the doctor: 'Dr Murphy told my mother that Father Charles suffered greatly in his last illness and that he was most wonderful in his patience. Dr Murphy had great admiration for Father Charles, especially on account of his patience and his piety' (Christina Frances O'Brien).

By this time, news of Charles' illness had spread throughout the city and, Father Eugene tells us, 'crowds of anxious inquirers continually besieged the Hall-door'.

Although he was still weak and helpless, Charles' condition became more stable for a time; on Christmas Eve Father Salvian noted that 'our dear Father Charles is not better, nor worse, but like a true Saint, he patiently carries his heavy cross'. The next day, Christmas Day, at eleven o'clock Father Norbert celebrated Mass in Charles' room. Father Norbert tells us that throughout his illness Charles' mind was always on God:

He was never once heard to utter a word of complaint though his sufferings were terrible in the extreme. He obeyed the physicians and infirmarian with the docility of a child and seemed to have no will but theirs. Yet during all these sufferings his mind was always united to God. Those long years of training produced their result in his soul. Even when towards the end he was unable to pronounce distinctly, the lips would move in prayer or the eyes would seek the crucifix near his bed.

A week later, Father Salvian's diary records a deterioration in Charles' condition:

31 December. Father Charles began to get worse yesterday and the

doctor gave no hope of his recovery. Today is just the same if not worse.

2 January. Dear Father Charles gets worse every day, but his patience in sufferings is indeed marvellous. *Salus infirmorum ora pro eo.*

3 January. Father Charles worse still.

On the night of 3 January, a male nurse came from Saint Vincent's Hospital to be with the religious who had been taking turns to watch Charles during the night. Father Eugene, who was one of those who, in his own words, vied with each other in their attendance in the sick room, wrote: 'What an example of patience did he not give to all during those days and nights! What willing obedience to our slightest wish!'

In the *Platea*, Father Norbert recorded the beginning of the last stage of Charles' earthly journey:

As the first few days of the new year passed away, it became more and more evident that no hope could be entertained of the recovery of Father Charles. Even the medical men who were constantly in attendance could give no assurance or hope; all they could say was, 'a few days at most'. On the afternoon of the Fourth, when the doctor called, a great change for the worse was visible, and then it was not days but hours. On the same day, 4 January, we learn from Father Salvian: 'It seems that the poor sick man has lost the power of speech and the sight of his eyes. He cannot swallow any food and seems to suffer very much, but no word of complaint ever escaped his lips.'

On Thursday, 5 January 1893, the Vigil of the Epiphany, Salvian wrote in his diary:

At a quarter past five, before going to say Mass, which I say every morning at six, I went to see Father Charles, and he appeared to be in his agony. The Infirmarian told me that Father Charles would die at about six, and so it happened, but I did not know till after my Mass that he was dead. Whilst I was vesting for Mass, I heard the sound of the community bell, and on my way to the Sacristy after Mass, Father Andrew, who was going to say the 6.30 Mass, told me that dear Father Charles was just gone.

Father Norbert tells us that Charles died at a quarter to six that morning:

The end was calm and peaceful. No struggle with death was evident, nor did any of those physical pains which are common at last moments manifest themselves. One last breath drawn with the same apparent ease and fullness as at any other time and the heart ceased to beat; his brethren waited for another sigh – it came not. The soul was with its God.

According to Father Eugene, with Charles when he died were a priest, two students and the nurse. Charles' death, he adds, 'was well in keeping with his life, quiet, unobtrusive, retiring, lived for God alone'.

At 7 p.m. the body of Father Charles was brought into the Church, accompanied by the whole of the community, with lighted candles, and singing the Miserere and the De Profundis, whilst the large bell was solemnly tolling. We found in the Church already a large number of people, waiting to see the body. Every one of them touched the hands or feet, the coffin being opened. The respect of the Irish to the Holy Priest, whoever he may be, is really remarkable, but the respect and veneration to our dear saintly Father Charles has been extraordinarily manifested at every occasion, but on this occasion it was indeed more than I can express in words.

The veneration shown by the people when Charles' body was brought to the church on the night of 5 January, described here by Father Salvian, was indeed extraordinary. Everyone seemed to know that Father Charles of Mount Argus had died, and all were intent on going to see him for the last time. A witness at the Apostolic Processes recalled the scene at Mount Argus that night:

Crowds hastened to the church when the news of his death spread. I went about 8 p.m. The church was full, and priests had to keep the crowds back, so great was the desire to touch the body which was exposed in the coffin. It took me an hour to make my way through the crowd up to the body and to get back again. As I returned home, I met crowds flocking up the church and asking us, 'Can the body be seen?'

The next day, 6 January, people were coming to the church all day long, as Father Salvian tells us:

From morning to late in the evening, there was a continual procession of hundreds, or rather thousands, of people going to see the dear Saint (as the people were saying). The whole day, but especially in the afternoon, the spacious church was filled with people. Two, and sometimes three and four, of our religious were near the coffin to protect it from the people, and to take from their hands books, rosaries, handkerchiefs … and touch the body of the deceased and give them back to them, to keep them as relics.

The following day, the weather was very cold and it began to snow, but this did not keep the crowds away; they still came in their thousands. On 8 January, which was a Sunday, the sermon at the High Mass was preached by Father Pius Devine, the subject being Father Charles' great virtues. One of those present recalled its effect: 'The preacher had known the servant of God for years, and was able to inform the immense congregation on many points unknown to the outer world, which possessed a thrilling interest, moving both preacher and audience to tears'. In the afternoon, at four o'clock, the Solemn Office of the Dead was sung by the members of the various Confraternities of the city: 'The spacious church was crammed everywhere by people and hundreds, or rather thousands, were outside, although fast raining and the mud half a foot deep' (Diary of Father Salvian). After the Office, the crowds began once more to file past the coffin. According to Father Wilfrid O'Hagan,

Such extraordinary crowds were never seen in Mount Argus. The people were from every corner of Ireland. The roads were blocked and it was absolutely impossible to get into the church without long waiting. Sunday evening was the wettest and most disagreeable here that I have seen for a long time. It was quite a Godsend that it was so else I am afraid some would have been smothered. Even as it was, the crowds were outside in the rain struggling to get in.

That night people continued to come to the church, 'all anxious to get a last glimpse of that face on which they loved to look, and to touch the body with some object of devotion' (Father Norbert McGettigan). 'For the space of five days', recalled Father Eugene Nevin, '"poor old Charlie", as he so often in life called himself, had the honours of a lying-in-state fit for a King or Emperor'.

On the morning of the funeral, 10 January, when the doctor and the undertakers went to close the coffin, they were surprised to find no trace of decomposition or rigor mortis. Father Wilfrid O'Hagan, who was then Provincial Consultor, describes the condition of the body in a letter written the day after the funeral:

He was five days lying in a church strongly heated with hotwater pipes and amid the suffocating atmosphere of the tens of thousands who from morning till night literally crammed the church. And yet there was not the slightest trace of decomposition, but his whole appearance was brighter and clearer than when alive. Nay more, the flesh on his forehead and hands remained quite soft; there was as little of the fixedness of death as if the blood were freely coursing in the veins. But more marvellous, the arms and hands and fingers were quite flexible when the coffin lid was screwed down. There was entirely absent the least appearance of the rigidity of death. Dr Murphy, who attended him, confesses that he could not explain it, for the immediate cause of death was of such nature that it would immediately cause rigidity.

It was Father Wilfrid who celebrated the Funeral Mass, which was attended by the auxiliary Bishop, Dr Donnelly, as Father Norbert tell us:

When the Office commenced at eleven o'clock the large church was packed to capacity, to its utmost containing capacity. The Most Rev. Dr Donnelly presided at the Office and Mass, at which Father Wilfrid, Consultor, was celebrant. Hundreds were obliged to remain outside during the Mass. The music of both Office and Mass was rendered by a choir of the secular priests from the city of whom there was a large number present, as well as the religious Orders, all of whom were represented. Very remarkable was the absence of any external manifestation of sorrow amongst the crowds present, as if by instinct the people preferred to pray *to* him rather than *for* him.

After the Mass, the Bishop led the prayers of Final Commendation and then the procession moved down the nave, towards the cemetery: 'In front walked the Sub-Deacon, carrying a cross, and accompanied by acolytes, after which the secular and regular clergy walked two by two; next in order was the celebrant of the High Mass, and last of all the members of the Confraternity of the Cross and Passion, bearing the coffin.' Slowly, the procession made its way through the crowd. A Passionist who was present at the funeral wrote, 'Inside the church, and away down the avenues, was one dense mass of human beings'; according to another eyewitness, as the body was being carried through the crowd, 'it seemed as if the people were about to snatch up the coffin and prevent the burial'. Fortunately, the Superintendent of the Dublin Metropolitan Police had sent a large number of officers to control the crowds outside the church; these now formed two rows and made a path through the crowd so that the procession could pass from the church to the cemetery. At the grave, the prayers were led by Father Wilfrid. When the last prayers were over, many of the people went back to the church, looking for some memento, as Father Eugene recalls:

The pall on which the coffin lay was touched with objects of devotion. The wax from the candles round the bier; even pieces of wood from the votive candle boxes were requisitioned as mementoes.

Anything in fact, if only remotely associated with Father Charles in life or death, had now a high value set upon it.

That evening, an account of the funeral was published in the *Evening Telegraph*:

Never before within living memory has there been such an outburst of religious sentiment and profound reverence as was beheld around the open grave of Father Charles. As the coffin was lowered into the grave, every eye was wet with tears, and loud and general manifestations of the most sincere regret went up from the multitude present, who clustered round with heads uncovered to take a last look at the coffin which enclosed the remains of a most exemplary and beloved priest.

'His death, like his life, was that of a saint': with these words of Father Dominic O'Neill our story began. Now we have reached its end which, as we said, is also a beginning. 'As the coffin was lowered into the grave', Charles' life took on a new and fuller meaning. His ministry now is not confined by space and time, and his compassion reaches out to all who turn to him in their need, whose lives are touched by his. The example of Saint Charles of Mount Argus is a lasting inspiration to all who are struggling to live according to the Gospel. The witness of a life lived generously in the service of God speaks more eloquently than any words, as Pope John Paul II affirmed: 'At a time like our own, characterised by a kind of allergy to belief in words not sustained by deeds, the witness of life remains the most important sign of credibility, because it accredits the sincerity of the apostle and the presence of the divine force working in him' (*L'Osservatore Romano*, 26 January 1987).

Blessed Charles witnessed to Christ not just by his words but by his life also. His compassion for the poor and the sick, his fidelity to prayer, his living faith and patience in suffering all testify to the fact that he was a true disciple of Christ crucified. Commenting on the life of Blessed Charles, one of the Theological Consultors of the Congregation for the Causes of Saints wrote:

We find ourselves here before a brilliant life, totally dedicated to the neighbour, especially the poor and the needy, and at the same time lived in retirement, in prayer, in perfect penance and obedience, leading to an intimate participation in the Passion of Christ.

It is in relation to the Passion of Christ that we come to understand the meaning of the life of Saint Charles. At his religious profession he committed himself to keeping alive in the hearts of God's people and in his own heart the memory of the Passion of Jesus. Commenting on this vow, Saint Paul of the Cross had written in the Rule:

Circumstances will open numerous other ways of promoting so great a work.... For the love of God is very ingenious, and is proved not so much by the words, as by the deeds and examples of the lovers.

Saint Charles' profound understanding of the intimate link between the Passion of Christ and human suffering opened for him a way of 'promoting so great a work', a way which manifests clearly the power of the Cross. As a true son of Saint Paul of the Cross, he lived in his own time and in his own particular way that gift of God which is the Passionist Vocation.

We are aware that the Passion of Christ continues in this world until He comes in glory; therefore, we share in the joys and sorrows of our contemporaries as we journey through life toward our Father. We wish to share in the distress of all, especially those who are poor and neglected; we seek to offer them comfort and to relieve the burden of their sorrow.

The power of the Cross, which is the wisdom of God, gives us strength to discern and remove the causes of human suffering.

For this reason, our mission aims at evangelizing others by means of the Word of the Cross. In this way, all may come to know Christ and the power of His resurrection, may share in His sufferings and, becoming like him in his death, may be united with Him in glory.

– Passionist Constitutions, 3

Appendices

Appendix One

After the death of Saint Charles, the Rector of Mount Argus wrote the customary obituary notice to send to the other Passionist communities. After giving a brief résumé of Charles' life, he went on to give this description of him:

Father Charles was a priest of singular piety and a religious who observed our Holy Rule with extraordinary fervour and exactness. Ever prompt in obedience, rigid in the observance of poverty, pure-minded in his actions, cherishing an ardent devotion to the Passion of our Divine Lord, and faithful son of the Congregation [of the Passion] in every respect, his life was like unto that of a Saint. Loving mortification and humiliation in whatever form they presented themselves, he grew daily in holiness so that the fame of his sanctity spread far and wide. A lover of seclusion constantly united with God in prayer, continually imploring the divine mercy for mankind, ready at all times to perform acts of charity towards his neighbour, Father Charles was looked up to as a typical Passionist. The people who venerated him as a saint flocked daily to Saint Paul's to obtain the holy man's blessing which not infrequently resulted in the cure of physical as well as moral ills. Never permitting himself to be distracted, but always remembering the presence of God – his mind unceasingly on things heavenly – his all-absorbing thought was the Sacred Passion of our Lord and the Dolours of Mary. As time grew apace, so did the love of God fructify in his soul so that his progress in virtue was marvellous. The holy names of Jesus and Mary were his favourite ejaculations, and he repeated them with such profound reverence that he touched the hearts of those that happened to be near him. He practised devotion to the Holy Souls in a heroic degree. So great was it, that he invariably asked those with whom he came in contact to intercede for their release. During the celebration of the Holy Sacrifice he generally exhibited signs of deep emotion, and it was not unusual for him to shed abundant tears. Living such a life of self-abnegation and increasing love of God – tending always to perfection – it is not to be wondered at that his death was such a holy and a happy one. Father Charles was not a preacher; but he did an incalculable amount of good for the salvation of souls by his burning exhortations to the groups who day by day came to seek his benedictions. God alone knows the benefits which have resulted to the Congregation as well as to the Church in general, from the humble prayers of this self-denying religious. Having celebrated Mass for the last time on the feast of the Immaculate Conception, he was stricken down on the following day by a painful illness, which increased daily more and more; but the holy man bore his sufferings in such a manner as to edify all. He breathed his last calmly and peacefully in the presence of his religious brethren at a quarter to six on Thursday morning, 5th of January. His death created intense sorrow, as was evidenced not only by his fellow-religious but by the public in general who came in thousands to St Paul's, anxious to get a last glimpse at him who during life was desirous of doing good to all without distinction of persons, and whose bright example not only excited the love of the faithful, but even won for him the admiration of those who differed from him in religion. Remembering the divine promises to the faithful religious we cannot but conclude that the reward of this devoted servant of God is 'exceeding great'.

Appendix Two

SERMON PREACHED BY FATHER WILFRID O'HAGAN CP
AT THE FUNERAL OF SAINT CHARLES
And Jesus went down to Nazareth and was subject to them (Luke 11:51)

I do not know if you have carefully thought of the significance of the silent life of our Lord, how he was for thirty years living in retirement and solitude, and only appeared twice in public: the first time, at the feast mentioned in today's Gospel [the feast of the Passover], and the second time, at the marriage in Cana of Galilee. Three years and a half, alone, was he doing the work of his ministry. One of the consequences of this: it shows that many live silently in this life – all those who are holy and come to God, who will rather stand by Divinity than scatter themselves over the earth.

This was the original spirit of the Church, which caused thousands upon thousands of men and women to bury themselves in the cloister. For they were dead to the world when the door of the cloister closed upon them. And so they thus worked alone, sleeping silently in their graves; and not until the final trumpet will it be seen or known, the work of their lives.

It is sad now for us today, to be gathered round the bier of one who loved us so long. He is a perfect saint: he lived for God alone, he thought nothing of himself, and his life was a perfect sacrifice. Upwards of forty years he has lived for God.

But to understand this thoroughly, I will give you a little information, of his mode of life. From the day he joined our Order and put on the habit he loved, he loved the observance of the sacred Rule, he loved the solitude of his cell, and solitude of his life. He never left the house, except under obedience, or on some work of charity. His work and his whole life was devoted to God; his whole charity was for anything that brought relief to the afflicted heart. His life was one of those superior beings, something

147

to be hidden away – he was nothing so far as he himself was concerned – outside the room wherein he found peace and solitude, and all those superior lights of heaven, which is only understood by those within the monastery.

No matter what went wrong in the world outside – all its changes and calamities – with him it was no concern; I don't believe he ever looked at a newspaper. If he was told anything that was sorrowful or evil, he would sigh for it, and would rejoice on hearing anything that was good. But no matter what storms or troubles might gather round, there was peace with God always standing in his soul. He lived superior to all those things. He lived according to the Rule laid down for him, and he had no ambition with the outside, hidden as he was in retirement.

His presence shed a light amongst us; he had humbled himself for God. And, what is more, it was not only this solitude of his own life, but all that ever knew him, never knew him to be without prayer – night and day; I almost think he prayed in his sleep. He prayed always; he prayed for those inside, and those who were outside; his whole life was a life of prayer.

He never asked for anything. His devotions were the most peculiar [i.e. particular]. He was most attentive to his religious duties and, though he might seem to have an aberration or want of recollection, I never knew him to forget anything of his religious duties. He had a special devotion to our Blessed Lady; when he was in pain, or anything troubled – it was to Mary. And so it was on the feast of the Immaculate Conception he said his last Mass. That evening he fell off his feet; he never rose from that moment, nearly four weeks ago, and it was only then we knew he had been suffering. He must have suffered immensely, and we never knew it. And even then, when we enquired, 'Are you in pain, Father Charles?', he would calmly answer, 'Not much'.

In the long period amongst us, he was never upbraided except for his zeal. I remember, forty years ago, he made some little mistake, and I heard the superior say, 'I have scolded that holy man, but I could now kneel down and kiss his feet'. Some men there are who seem a saint to those outside, but he was a saint to those inside. He was an example to us all.

I will not detain you; it is hard to retain ourselves when speaking of one whose charity was so much – and given with every zeal that was possible – if he thought he could assist in any way to comfort those who were in grief or sorrow, and brush away their tears, or do what he could to relieve their sufferings. Another thing: he was never known yet to say an uncharitable word against anyone, and that is more than can be said of the greatest saints, except Saint John. If he heard others speak uncharitably, he would plead an excuse in his own quiet way, so that he might turn the shafts of anger, or deaden the sound of scandal. Such a life is a curiosity in this nineteenth century. There may be holy men, beautiful priests they may be, and great scholars, but simple bodily and holy charity the Lord has taken from us. And when shall we look upon his like again!

It was not until he died, did we feel the treasure we had lost. I suppose there is not a single man or woman in Ireland who has not heard of him. He preached by the holiness of his life. He preached by his charity and by his holiness far better than all the priests in Ireland, and, I will say, he will preach better after his death. Let us pray to God to receive that holy man, after his life of solitude and suffering, to rejoice in the Kingdom of Heaven.

Appendix Three

The cure of Mrs Spaetgens took place in 1952. At that time it was investigated by the ecclesiastical authorities of the diocese of Roermond as being possibly miraculous. However their findings could not be presented to the Congregation for the Cause of Saints until Charles was declared Venerable in 1979. The documents were then investigated by the medical experts in Rome and, with their approval, the *Positio super miraculo*, a document of over two hundred pages of medical evidence, was presented to the Holy Father on 21 November 1987, paving the way for the Beatification of Father Charles of Mount Argus.

The short account of the miraculous cure of Mrs Spaetgens which follows was made from the original documents by Sister Mary Woodhall LCM.

Mrs Octavia Spaetgens, born in Holland in October 1880, enjoyed good health until 1950 when, during a visit to Lourdes, she suffered her first liver colic. This was repeated about a month later, accompanied by fever.

The doctors diagnosed 'Cholecystitis with calculi' (inflammation of the gall bladder and gall stones). They advised surgical intervention.

Mrs Spaetgens was admitted to hospital on August 27 1951 and a few days later underwent surgery and a cholecystectomy was performed. Forty calculi were extracted.

Three or four days after the operation the patient complained of violent abdominal pains accompanied by alimentary and digestive problems.

The patient developed pneumonia and later became jaundiced. Medical treatment was given and Mrs Spaetgens was discharged from the hospital on 1 November. At home medical treatment was continued and was efficacious until a few days before Christmas when the patient was re-admitted to Hospital with violent pains in the upper abdomen. In spite

152

of treatment the pains, accompanied by fever, persisted and there was a serious decline in the patient's general condition.

A barium enema was performed and showed the presence of a downward displacement of the left colic flexure caused by a mass in the left hypochondrium. The mass was easily palpable, fixed and very painful. The doctors decided against surgical intervention on account of the patient's age and general condition. Mrs Spaetgens was discharged home in a serious state on 19 January 1952. The prognosis was unfavourable and limited in time.

At home the pains, the vomiting and general decline in the patient's condition continued. On the third night, the patient's condition became critical; she was agitated and disturbed by continuous vomiting. During that night Mrs Spaetgens invoked the intercession of Father Charles of Saint Andrew. She became immediately calmer; she felt suddenly cured. The vomiting ceased and the bowel activity became normal so there was no longer need for the frequent enemas. The patient began to eat normally, enjoying some fairly indigestible foods.

Mrs Spaetgens' general condition began to improve. The doctors were informed a few days after this event occurred and were able to observe the progressive disappearance of the mass in the left hypochondnum. The lady died twenty-two years later at the age of ninety four. She had no return of the symptoms.

Several doctors expressed their opinion as to what had occurred, but even when they felt able to explain the gradual disappearance of the mass in natural terms of reabsorption or drainage into the digestive tract, they were unanimous in considering the sudden restoration of the intestinal canalisation as an extraordinary event: 'Confirming the extraordinary nature, the cure came about rapidly, interrupting what had been the constantly unfavourable course of a state of ill-health which had lasted for months'.

Sister Mary Woodall LCM

Appendix Four

The cure of Mr Dormans took place in 1999. The findings of the Diocesan Tribunal were sent to Rome and, after preliminary examination, were examined by the Medical Council of the Congregation for the Causes of Saints on 24 November 2005. It was unanimously agreed that the case should be submitted to the theologians of the same Congregation as a possible miracle worked through the intercession of Blessed Charles of Mount Argus. With the favourable votes of the theologians, followed by the approval of the cardinals and bishops of the Congregation of the Causes of Saints, Pope Benedict XVI authorised the Prefect of the same Congregation, Cardinal José Saraiva Martins, on 16 December 2006 to promulgate the Decree on the Miracle of Blessed Charles of Mount Argus, leading to his canonisation.

Adolf (Dolf) Dormans was born on 29 August 1926. He lived in the village of Munstergeleen in the Netherlands where Saint Charles Houben was born. His medical history included a gastric ulcer and surgery for repair of an inguinal hernia and an intervertebral prolapse.

On 27 March 1999 he began to experience abdominal pains. These became progressively worse. An attending doctor suspected intestinal obstruction. An x-ray on 29 March showed dilatation of both small and large bowel. Paralysis of the bowel was diagnosed. Mr Dormans was admitted to Maasland Hospital in Sittard where he underwent emergency surgery. During the operation a gangrenous, perforated appendix with associated generalised peritonitis were discovered. The surgeon carried out an appendicectomy and lavage of the peritoneal cavity. As the abdomen was very distended, the wound was not sutured; a drain was inserted and the wound covered with a plastic sheet (called a Bogotà bag). The patient was then transferred to the Intensive Care unit.

It was necessary to repeat the peritoneal lavage several times during the following days because of persistent infection. Pus, bile and faecal matter had continued to collect in the peritoneal cavity. Despite these interventions, the bowels remained distended, the peritonitis persisted and the patient's condition continued to deteriorate.

On 11 April the abdomen was explored once more. This revealed several intestinal perforations which were leaking bilious matter; two abscesses were discovered. The small intestine was very swollen and friable. After the intestinal lesions had been repaired, another peritoneal lavage was carried out and a further plastic sheet applied over the wound. As a result of these complications, a fistula formed between the small bowel and the skin.

After these interventions the situation remained grave. The family was informed by the surgeon that the prognosis was extremely poor. The patient's case was deemed hopeless and a decision was made that in the event of cardiac arrest he should not be resuscitated. Mr Dormans was given the Sacrament of the Sick.

In spite of the antibiotics, transfusions and feeding catheter (into a large neck vein), his condition deteriorated. His situation was complicated by pneumonia and heart problems. This was the patient's state on 11 April 1999.

Dolf Dormans himself tells us what happened next: 'From the beginning, I had entrusted myself to Blessed Father Charles, praying to him for a good outcome from my illness and asking him to bless the hands of the doctors who were taking care of me. On 11 April 1999, my nephew Simon's First Communion day, my wife Maria and my children were informed by Doctor Strouken at about 3.00 PM that my situation was very serious and that, from the medical point of view, there was nothing more to be done: they were told, then, to prepare themselves for my death. On the same day I received the Sacraments and made my last farewell to my wife, my children and their spouses, my nephews and nieces, my three brothers and my sister. As I have a great devotion to Blessed Father Charles, I prayed asking him to be close to me in this very difficult time.'

Throughout his illness, Mr Dormans had kept in his hand a relic of Father Charles given to the family for him by Father Joachim Van der Heijden CP. His son Martin says: 'I was deeply impressed by the profound faith my father had in Father Charles; he told me: "I am putting my life in Father Charles' hands, but I would prefer to remain here"'.

The next day, Monday 12 April, Martin Dormans went to make arrangements for his father's funeral as his father had instructed him to do.

However, on the same day, there was an unexpected improvement in his father's condition which continued steadily until finally, after 107 days in hospital, 58 of which were spent in Intensive Care, he was discharged on 14 July 1999.

As the fistula was still present, nutrition continued to be given through the feeding catheter while at home. He was admitted once more to hospital on 27 July because the feeding catheter had become infected. Therefore, it was removed. Feeding by intestinal means (through the fistula) was initiated. On 26 October he was again admitted to hospital. The fistula was excised and intestinal continuity was re-established. After a few days he began normal feeding and was discharged on 8 November 1999.

Subsequently, Mr Dormans was examined by medical experts who concluded that he was in good health and free of any continuing ill effects. His good health has continued to this day. In addition to what was affirmed by relatives and friends at the Diocesan Tribunal, all the medical staff who spoke at the Tribunal agreed upon the exceptional character and scientific inexplicability of Mr Dormans' cure.

The original diagnosis was perforated, gangrenous appendicitis with general peritonitis and multi-organ failure in a patient of 71 years with prolonged septicaemia and agonal state. There was a sudden and unexpected resolution of the agonal state and of the general clinical condition; a favourable course of the whole abdominal pathology; a complete and lasting cure with no long-term adverse consequences.

Maureen Catherwood and Dr Michael Cameron

Sources and Bibliography

Unpublished Sources

ARCHIVES OF HOLY CROSS RETREAT, ERE, BELGIUM

Registre de nos SS. Ministères de 1841 à 1872.
Membres de la Communauté (d'Ere) arrivées et départs de 1840 à 1931.
Administration de la Maison d'Ere de 1840 à 1866.
Registre des Visites Canoniques.

ARCHIVES OF THE PROVINCE OF SAINT GABRIEL, BELGIUM

Registre du Noviciat d'Ere 1840–1856.
Origine di questa fondazione (d'Ere) 1840–1868.
Les Passionistes en Belgique (typescript).
Platea du Père Seraphin (microfilm).

ARCHIVES OF THE PROVINCE OF SAINT JOSEPH, ENGLAND

General Administration Book of Saint Wilfrid's Retreat, Cotton Hall 1850–1854.
General Administration Book of Saint Wilfrid's Retreat, Cotton Hall 1854–1858.
Mission Book (Parish Register) of Saint Wilfrid's, Cotton.
Missæ pro Populo quæ celebrantur in Ecclesia S. Wilfridi 1850-1858.
Platea of Saint Michael's Retreat, Aston Hall.
Register of Arrivals and Departures, Saint Saviour's Retreat, Broadway.
Platea of Saint Joseph's Retreat, London.
General Administration Book of Saint Joseph's Retreat, The Hyde, and Saint Joseph's
    Retreat, Highgate, London 1852-1859.
General Administration Book of Saint Joseph's Retreat, Highgate, London 1871–
Diary of Father Ignatius Spencer (3 vols).
Letter of Father Ignatius Spencer to Father Eugene Martorelli, 24 April 1852.
Obituary of Father Charles (Houben) of Saint Andrew.

ARCHIVES OF SAINT PAUL'S RETREAT, MOUNT ARGUS, DUBLIN, IRELAND

Account of the Foundation of the Retreat of Blessed Paul of the Cross, Harold's Cross,
    near Dublin 1856 (Platea 1856–1899).
Register of Arrivals and Departures, Saint Paul's Retreat, Mount Argus 1856–1874.
Register of Passionists, Anglo-Hibernian Province of Saint Joseph.
Annals of the Anglo-Hibernian Province (4 vols).

Chronicles of the Novitiate of Saint Saviour's Retreat, Broadway 1864–1867.
Chronicles of the Novitiate of Saint Saviour's Retreat, Broadway 1867–1871.
Diary of Father Salvian Nardocci 1855–1896 (19 vols).
Newspaper cuttings collected by Father Salvian Nardocci (2 vols).
Diary of Confrater Adrian Cole 1885–1886.
Circular Letter of the Most Rev. Father Bernard Mary of Jesus, Superior General, on the conclusion of the Visitation of the Province of Saint Joseph, 31 August 1879.
Circular Letter of the Most Rev. Father Bernard Mary of Jesus, Superior General, to all the religious of the Province of Saint Joseph, 28 November 1885.
Obituary of Father Jerome (Smith) of the Purification.

ARCHIVES OF THE VICE POSTULATOR, SAINT PAUL'S RETREAT, MOUNT ARGUS

Sermon preached by Father Wilfrid O'Hagan at the funeral of Father Charles.
An Appreciation of Father Charles by his confessor, Father Norbert (McGettigan) of Saint Paul of the Cross.
Personal Recollections of Father Charles by Father Eugene Nevin (typescript).
Personal Impressions of Father Charles at Ardoyne, Belfast, by P. J. Tiernan.

GENERAL ARCHIVES, SANCTI GIOVANNI E PAOLO, ROME

Atti delle Consulte Generali 1870-1909.
Report on the Visitation of the Province of Saint Joseph by Father Alphonsus (O'Neill) of the Blessed Virgin Mary, 5 December 1878.
Letter of Father Alphonsus O'Neill to Father Bernard Mary Silvestrelli, 14 August 1878.

ARCHIVES OF THE POSTULATION, SANCTI GIOVANNI E PAOLO, ROME

Meditations, Sermons and Prayers of Father Charles of Saint Andrew (manuscript written in his own hand, p. 113).
Exemplar authenticum epistolarum servi Dei P. Carolia a S. Andrea (79 letters written by Charles to members of his family).

These documents were formerly in the Archives of the Congregation for the Causes of Saints and were transferred to the Archives of the Postulation on 8 January 1988.

DUBLIN DIOCESAN ARCHIVES

Ordinary Process of Dublin 1928-1929.
Apostolic Process of Dublin 1936-1938.

Published Sources

Articles for the Apostolic Process of the Servant of God Father Charles of Saint Andrew, Passionist, Dublin, 1936.

Positio super virtutibus S. D. Caroli a S. Andrea, Roma, 1955.

Nova Positio super virtutibus S. D. Caroli a S. Andrea, Roma, 1972.

Relatio et Vota Congressus peculiaris super virtutibus S. D. Caroli a S. Andrea, Roma, 1978.

Positio super miraculo (Canonizationis Ven. S. D. Caroli a S. Andrea) Roma, 1987.

Regulæ et Constitutiones Congr. Sanctissimæ Crucis et Passionis D.N.J.C., a cura di F. Giorgini (Fontes Historicæ Congregationis Passionis, I), Roma, 1958.

Rule and Constitutions of the Congregation of the Passion of Jesus Christ, San Gabriele (Teramo), 1984.

Paolo della Croce, Lettere, a cura di Amedeo della Madre del Buon Pastore (4 vol.) Roma, 1924.

Paolo della Croce, La Congregazione dela Passione de Gesù: cos'è e cosa vuole, a cura di F. Giorgini (Ricerche di storia e spiritualità passionista, I) Roma, 1978.

Journal Historique et Littéraire (Liège), VIII, 1 May 1841.

Bibliography

Abbot, Walter A. (Ed.), *The Documents of Vatican II*, London, Geoffrey Chapman, 1972.

Austin, Father, *The Life of Father Charles of the Congregation of the most holy Cross and Passion of our Lord Jesus Christ*, Dublin, Sealy, Bryers & Walker, 1893.

Bonifacius, Pater, *De Dienaar Gods, p. Carolus Houben van de congregatie der passionisten*, Brugge, Desclée de Brouwer, 1929 (English translation in the Archives of the Vice-Postulator, Mount Argus, Dublin).

Brovetto, Costante, *Introduzione alla spiritualità di S. Paolo della Croce*, S. Gabriele (Teramo), Edizioni 'Eco', 1955.

Burke, Edmund, 'Carlo di S. Andrea', *Bibliotheca Sanctorum*, Roma, Istituto Giovanni XXIII, 1961 (20 vol.), Vol. III, col. 800-801.

Charles, Conrad, *The Foundation of the Passionists in England 1840-1851* (Unpublished Doctoral Thesis, P.U.G.), Roma, 1961.

Christopher, Father, *Father Charles of Mount Argus*, Dublin, M. H. Gill & Son, 1938

Devine, Pius, *Life of the Very Rev. Father Dominic of the Mother of God* (Barberi), Passionist, London, R. Washbourne, 1898.

Devine, Pius, (Pius a Sp. Sancto), *Life of Father Ignatius of Saint Paul*, Passionist (The Hon. & Rev. George Spencer), Dublin, James Duffy, 1866.

Edmond, Pater, *Leven van den Dienaar Gods, Pater Carolus Houben, passionist*, Mook, Klooster Mater Dolorosa, 1923 (English translation in the Archives of the Vice Postulator, Mount Argus, Dublin).

John Paul II, P.P., 'Address to Catholic Action of Rome', *L'Osservatore Romano*, weekly edition in English, 26 January 1987, p. 11.

Kelly, Oliver, 'Witnessing to God', *The Cross*, 68 (April 1978), pp. 16-20.

Menegazzo, Federico, 'An ecumenical soul: Venerable Charles Houben CP' *L'Osservatore Romano*, weekly edition in English, 24 January 1983, pp. 10-11.

Menegazzo, Federico, *Il Beato Domenico della Madre di Dio*, Roma, Postulazione dei PP. Passionisti, 1963.

Mercurio, Roger & Rouse, Silvan (Eds.), *Words from the Heart – A Selection from the Personal Letters of Saint Paul of the Cross*, Dublin, Gill and Macmillan, 1976.

Molinari, Paul, 'The Theology of Canonization', *The Way Supplement*, 38 (Winter 1980), pp. 7–13.

Molinari, Paul, 'Tradition and Saints' Lives', *The Way*, 21 (1981), pp. 123-36.

Munstergeleen – Een Monografie Over Een Limburgse Gemeente, 1970.

Ravasi, Ladislao, *La Congregazione dei Passionisti verso la metà del secolo* XIX, Caravate, Edizioni Madonna del Sasso, 1963.

Smith, Joseph, *Paul Mary Pakenham, Passionist*, London and Edinburgh, Sands, 1915

Spencer, Paul Francis (Ed.), *Letters of Father Charles of Mount Argus to his Family*, Dublin, Passionist Publications, 1985.

Spencer, Paul Francis, 'Sharing in the Sufferings of Jesus – The Spirituality of Saint Paul of the Cross', *Religious Life Review*, 20 (1981), pp. 147-53.

Wilson, Alfred, *Blessed Dominic Barberi*, London, Sands, 1967.

Young, Urban, *Life of Father Ignatius Spencer* CP, London, Burns, Oates & Washbourne, 1933.

Young, Urban, *Life and Letters of the Venerable Father Dominic* (Barberi) CP, London, Burns, Oates & Washbourne, 1926.

Young, Urban, *Venerable Dominic Barberi in England*, London, Burns, Oates & Washbourne, 1935.

Herald of Hope

Reflections on the Life & Spirit of Saint Charles of Mount Argus

ISBN 978-1-905965-01-4

What can someone who died over a hundred years ago possibly say to us today? Saint Charles of Mount Argus died in Dublin in 1893. Can his life speak to people who live in a very different world? These reflections on Charles' life and spirit attempt to allow him to dialogue with us, to share with us his sense of what it means to be a disciple of Jesus Christ.

Contributors: Martin Coffey CP, Brian D'Arcy CP, Frank Keevins CP, Paul Francis Spencer CP, Aidan Troy CP, Ignatius Waters CP.

Forthcoming Titles

Saint Charles of Mount Argus: Historical Papers

ISBN 978-1-905965-05-2

Letters of Saint Charles to his Family

ISBN 978-1-905965-03-8

Saint Charles Prayer Book

ISBN 978-1-905965-04-5

AVAILABLE FROM MUNGO BOOKS

Mungo Books is an imprint of Ovada Books devoted
to publications of Scottish Catholic interest.

A Cairn of Small Stones
John Watts
ISBN 1-905965-00-1

This is a tale of the West Highlands in the eighteenth century, told as
the autobiography of a tenant farmer of North Morar. As Ian More
McLellan recounts his life story we are carried through ninety dramatic
years – through the risings of 1715 and 1745 and their aftermath, the
famines of the '70s and '80s, the emigrations to the New World and the
breaking up of the old clan society.

  These form the backdrop to his own daily family life as son, husband,
father and grandfather, and as a farmer who also turned his hand to
droving, lead mining and sea-fishing.

An exceedingly well framed novel … [with] immense feeling for
the land and its people. A scholarly work, but written by a man too
informed to be patronising, too compassionate not to leave his reader
with a sense of magic of the glen and the strength of its people.

– *The Catholic Times*

John Watts is the author of several works of history, including: *Scalan: The Forbidden College 1716–1799* (1999), *Hugh MacDonald: Highlander, Jacobite & Bishop* (2002) and *A Canticle of Love: The Story of the Franciscan Sisters of the Immaculate Conception* (2006).

Eilein na h-Òige: The Poems of Father Allan McDonald
edited by Ronald Black
ISBN 1-901157-61-x

The name of Father Allan McDonald (Maighstir Ailein), 1859–1905,
is evergreen in the Gaelic-speaking islands of Uist, Barra and Eriskay.
A native of Fort William, he wore himself out in the service of his
parishioners at Daliburgh, and was transferred in 1894 to Eriskay, his
beloved *Eilein na h-Òige* ('Isle of Youth'). Among his labours was the
publication of a Gaelic hymnal which Ronald Black, the editor, has
combined selections of in this volume with 27 poems first published
in 1965, providing a resulting body of some 60 items with an English
translation, introduction and notes.

A priceless treasure
– *Flourish*

A very valuable mine of information on Father Allan and Catholic
Gaeldom
– Abbot Mark Dilworth

Ronald Black is Gaelic editor of *The Scotsman* and the Uist newspaper *Am Pàipear*. He
has published *An Tuil: Anthology of 20th Century Scottish Gaelic Verse* (1999), *Smuain-
tean fo Éiseabhal* (2000) the poetry of Dòmhnall Aonghais Bhàin of South Uist, and *An
Lasair: Anthology of 18th Century Scottish Gaelic Verse* (2001).

Ovada Books, an activity of the Passionists in Scotland and Ireland, has as its aims the promotion of Catholic faith and culture; supporting the ministry of the Passionists; and helping people to understand the Catholic Faith through publishing, retailing and other means.

If you would like further information on how you can help our work, please contact us at

Ovada Books
Saint Mungo's Retreat
52 Parson Street
Glasgow
G4 0RX

Tel/Fax +44 (0)141 552 5523

Scottish Charity Number sco 15760
The Passionists

xxii viii
Ann.Dō
mmvii
Set in
DTL Elzevir
xi × xiv × xxiii
by Gerard Daniëls,
based on fonts by
Christoffel van Dijck